NEGATIVE SPLITS

A MIDDLE-AGED, NEWBIE RUNNER'S JOURNEY TO THE FIRST MARATHON

DAVID M. WHITE

August 17, 2022

"You have to go out.
You don't have to come back."
— Motto of the Massachusetts Humane Society

Viv,

Facing down fears is the first step in daring to be great.

Thank you for your support and understanding, especially when I least deserved either.

Love,
Dave

CONTENTS

PRAISE FOR NEGATIVE SPLITS

"Gritty, honest, tongue-in-cheek, colorful – this is a story about falling in love with long-distance running, by a now-prominent runner who started out as a confirmed couch potato."

—Patricia Nell Warren, *New York Times* Best-Selling Author of *The Front Runner*

"*David White proves that it's all about making the decision to put on your shoes, do the work, and go for it. In the marathon – or in life – it's the same. Some sit and watch, the others participate. Guess which is transformational?*"

—Kathrine Switzer, Winner, 1974 New York City Marathon, Author of *Marathon Woman*

"David White's story of reclamation rings true for any runner who has struggled through injury and defeat and come back strong. His writing is on the mark and will resonate with runners at all levels who realize that running is a gift to be treasured. His story will motivate readers to stay true to their goals and find inspiration to keep putting one foot in front of the other, as he did, to cross the finish line."

—Gail Kislevitz, Author of *First Marathons: Personal Encounters with the 26.2-Mile Monster*

"A setback constitutes a setup for a stronger comeback. David White's inspirational journey exemplifies this concept on many different levels and is transferable to all athletes, especially marathon runners. This is a must-read for all runners motivated to reach new levels within their own personal journey. Enjoy the ride!"

—Sid Howard, Winner of 5 Masters World Championships, 50 United States National Championships, Holder of 5 World Records and 6 United States Records

"Wouldn't it be great if White's work motivated Americans to get up off the couch? We all would love to run a negative split again. Just remember what's important: NEVER STOP RUNNING."

—Gary Muhrcke, Winner of the Inaugural New York City Marathon (1970)

FOR JENNIFER L. WHITE, ESQ.:
INTIMIOR INTIMO MEO

EPIGRAPH

Negative Splits:

(n) To run the second half of a race faster than the first half.

PREFACE

NOT ALL VICTORIES come with medals.

Prior to my 40th birthday, running a marathon was not a priority for me. In fact, the concept held no charm.

Like most Americans, I was indifferent to distance running. As a New Yorker, I had a cursory familiarity with the annual spectacle which snarls our streets on the first Sunday in November. If I serendipitously stumbled upon the event while flipping through television channels from the sedentary comfort of my couch, I watched a few minutes of coverage until I grew bored.

"What sane person would do that to himself?" I momentarily pondered before slathering more hollandaise sauce on my Eggs Benedict and stirring the celery stalk in a spicy Bloody Mary.

Life has a funny way of changing your perspective.

Negative Splits chronicles my conversion from committed couch potato to multi-event USA Track & Field Masters All-American.

I invested more than 10 months to prepare for my first marathon. During that period I dropped a significant amount of weight (42lbs) and effectively took on a non-paid, part-time job which materially altered my social life. By Marathon Sunday, I was in peak physical condition.

There is a difference between expectation and hope. A pregnant woman expects to deliver a child. She may harbor a hope that the newborn will be of a particular gender. The distinction is similarly useful when contemplating a marathon.

I expected to break 4:00:00 in my marathon debut performance. My hope was to register a finishing time fast enough to qualify for the Boston Marathon®, the world-class event which is every distance runner's dream.

Let's look at this by the numbers. Statistics reveal that less than 0.5% of the United States population has attempted to run a marathon. The overwhelming majority of those athletes will complete the course.

Then there are others.

Before retiring for bed the night before the 2010 ING˚ NYC Marathon, my wife, Jennifer, sought to assuage my anxiety.

"Regardless of what happens, you'll forever have a finishing time that begins with a '3,'" she opined.

There are certain outcomes in life for which we make no allowance because they are seemingly absurd on their face. Like the unsinkable RMS Titanic not arriving at New York's Pier 54, the cursed Chicago Cubs winning the World Series, or Keith Richards living to see his 70th Birthday.

The work you hold in your hands is a first-person account of an anomalous result, the often untold story of a forgotten minority.

Sometimes the deity is in the details, and humanity is in the retelling.

While the account I share is unique, I am the Everyman, the placeholder for archetypal running experiences. Those who are preparing to compete in their first marathon may profit from the tale. Seasoned competitors are likely to recognize themselves in the universality of the narrative.

Thank you for your decision to purchase this work. More poignantly, I appreciate your investment of the most precious non-renewable resource: time. Please enjoy *Negative Splits*. I welcome your feedback at dmw@negativesplitsbook.com.

PART I:
The Journey Begins

"If you want to win something, run 100 meters. If you want to experience something, run a marathon."

—1952 Three-Time Olympic Gold Medalist Emil Zatopek

I PREFACE THIS ACCOUNT by confessing that I am among the most unlikely of individuals to pen a running memoir. I was not predisposed to mark miles. I took no pleasure from pounding pavement. Mine was the sedentary lifestyle, a comfortable routine of eating what I wanted, when I wanted. I looked upon the weekend warriors who strode up and down the Lower Manhattan Esplanade with a mixture of ridicule and open contempt. It seemed to me that unless one is being chased, there is no point to running.

It wasn't always that way. I was a former athlete of modest accomplishments. In July 1981, I ran my first 5k, an event commemorating the 75th Anniversary of the founding of my hometown, River Vale, NJ.

In the autumn of 1984, I entered my freshman year at St. Joseph Regional High School in Montvale, NJ. Standing 5'00" and weighing 95lbs, I was too small for football. Our Cross Country squad consisted of boys who looked like me. The upperclassmen claimed that my new sport would be great if I enjoyed throwing up after every practice and performing without spectators.

Undeterred, I returned home each night too tired to eat or to do homework.

We finished the season 5-2-0 in dual meets. Despite that success, my competitive passion was elsewhere. In November, I reported to ice hockey captain's practice at 88lbs and a resolve to never again run more than 2.5 miles.

In my sophomore year, I turned my attention to track & field. I became a 100m, 200m specialist. A teammate of mine, Rich Harrington, became one of the premier schoolboy milers in New Jersey. He described me as "quick," a label consonant with my physical appearance.

I never hit the weight room and consequently lacked the definition in my thighs and upper body that is typical of true speed merchants. Nonetheless, I held my own against contemporaries whose accomplishments still stand among the Garden State's greatest. My shining moment occurred during the 1988 Bergen County Meet of Champions. I came in fourth of five runners in what was then the second fastest 200m heat in Bergen County history. While I got smoked by three blurs that overtook me before I reached the top of the turn, I remain proud that I handily bested the entrant from Paramus Catholic.

Four months later I reported to Fordham University as a walk-on to the Men's Track & Field Team. I was honored to participate at the Division I level but was hamstrung by the many distractions that come with living away from home for the first time.

An ankle injury in December sabotaged my training and I competed in a single 60m race at Southern Connecticut State University's James W. Moore Field House. Our team subsequently won the 1989 New York State Collegiate Track Conference Indoor Championship, an accomplishment to which I made no contribution due to injury.

The outdoor season produced equally disappointing results. In the spring of 1989, Harrington, struggling with a knee injury sustained at Drexel University, and I reunited on a cold, rain-drenched afternoon at Columbia University's Baker Athletics Complex. Compared to the scholarship talent on the track, my 100m performance was as lackluster as my former teammate's middle distance effort. That event more than any other motivated my decision to step away from collegiate athletics and embark upon a decade of full-time employment with United Parcel Service® that ran concurrent with the remainder of my undergraduate and graduate studies.

Thus began my 20-year period of self-imposed of athletic exile.

MY WIFE, JENNIFER, did not grow up with a passion for running. A former state champion high school tennis player, she became easily winded following physical exertion. A quarter-mile jog would redden her face and frustrate her spirit. In September 2007 she decided to do something to better her conditioning.

Working with personal trainer Meaghan Shea several mornings a week soon built strength and improved Jennifer's cardio endurance. She ran the Big Brothers/Big Sisters of NYC RBC 5k "Race for the Kids" in Manhattan's Riverside Park and was pleased with the result. The following spring she built a base before joining Team for Kids ("TFK"), the official charity of the New York Road Runners ("NYRR").

When Jennifer told me she planned to run the 2009 ING New York City Marathon, I thought she was crazy. We were attorneys, not endurance athletes. But to my utter amazement, she remained faithful to the thrice-a-week group training schedule. On alternating nights, she would leave our apartment in Battery Park City to run alone. Upon her return she would find me as she had left me: on the sofa. When I inquired where she had run, Jennifer would matter-of-factly remark that she had gone up to Times Square, an 8-mile roundtrip trek. I would simply shake my head in dumbstruck awe, believing I could never match the feat.

Jennifer also made a new group of "running buddies." These included Matt Martinez, MD, a pediatric cardiologist, his energy project consultant wife, Sondra, and their close friend, Stephanie Pianka, a financial management executive.

TFK orchestrated a number of social events for its members and their significant others. I explained to Jennifer that I had no interest in being around people who were obsessed with running. I liken the experience to being the designated driver at the frat house kegger. If you have no shared field of experience with your social companions, the interaction will likely degenerate into antisocial awkwardness.

At one point I became so boorish as to tell Jennifer, "If they begin to talk about running, I'm going to get up and leave." She thought I was joking. I assured her I was not.

On October 1, 2009 *New York Times* health blogger Tara Parker-Pope included Jennifer in a profile of first-time marathoners running through pain. Jennifer struggled through an iliotibial ("I.T.") band injury.

The connective tissue runs along the outer edge of the leg and provides stabilization to the knee. Inflammation in that region is one of the most common, and frustrating, injuries to plague distance runners.

Faced with the choice to defer entry until the 2010 ING Marathon or risk further injury that year, Jennifer opted to gut it out, a decision which surprised no one who knows her.

The Thursday before the 2009 ING NYC Marathon we attended the Expo at the Jacob K. Javits Convention Center. I could not imagine a place I would less rather be. I walked amid row after row of marathon apparel. Foreign women dispensed with the decorum of changing rooms and stripped down to their bras and panties in the middle of the floor. Collectively, this was truly a breed onto themselves.

As a peace offering, Jennifer bought me a shirt that depicts two Pac-Man™-esque figures. The text bubble above the first's head says "Marathon, Marathon, Marathon …", while the other figure has x-ed out eyes and a "ZZZZZ" text bubble above its head. No memento could have more accurately captured my feelings.

Three days later, Jennifer completed the 40th New York City Marathon, her first attempt at that distance. She proudly wore her Finisher's Medal to the restaurant where we celebrated the feat with family and friends. She also wore the recognition to her law firm the next day. I took solace in the belief that our lives would return to some semblance of normalcy as the marathon faded into memory.

I was wrong.

JENNIFER CONTINUED TO BASK in the post-race afterglow. Thanksgiving came and went. Christmas passed by as well. On New Year's Eve, she shared another fond reminiscence of the marathon. And for reasons I have yet to identify, that was the straw that figuratively broke my back.

At 8:20pm I unilaterally decided that we would scrap our plans in favor of the Emerald Nuts® Midnight Run, a 4-mile jaunt in Central Park.

Now it was Jennifer's time to opine that *I* was crazy. I had not run a mile that year. I did not own compression tights, a technical shirt, or any item of moisture-wicking apparel. What I did have was the gut you'd expect to find on a 40-year old who lugged around nearly 30lbs over the classic Body Mass Index.

Dressed in multiple layers of non-breathable clothing and wearing running shoes that had long since passed their prime, I looked like Rocky Balboa, circa 1977.

We made it to the New York Road Runners office shortly before 9:00pm and registered for the run.

Amid the freezing rain and ice-slicked pavement we toed the line with nearly 4,000 other revelers. At the stroke of Midnight, fireworks exploded above Cherry Hill and we were off.

The first mile wasn't all that taxing. The festive mood, music and adrenaline all helped to distract me. The euphoria soon ended as reality set in at Cat Hill, a relatively slight incline. My breathing became labored and the sweat drenched my under layer and the hair beneath my woolen cap.

As I recall our pace never broke 11:00 per mile. With each successive step I spoke less and struggled more.

At Mile 3 I saw a bright light ahead. Understanding it could not be the Finish Line, I grew confused. As we approached the source, I realized to my shock and horror that it was a camera crew.

CNN correspondent Gary Tuchman and his 11-year old daughter, Samantha, were running the course. The network cut live to the pair at each mile marker. Earlier in the broadcast he remarked, "On New Year's Eve, tourists go to Times Square. Real New Yorkers run in Central Park."

It was my unfortunate luck to draw even with the journalist and his pint-sized inspiration as CNN once again cut live to the run. Tuchman thrust a microphone at us and asked how we were doing. Unable to form a sentence but unwilling to look like a fool on national television, I flashed a confident "thumbs up" and hoped that my drawn hoodie would prevent identification.

We picked up the pace.

With about 600m to go on the West Drive downhill that parallels The Pond, I was spent. I cast a glance across my chest and asked Jennifer what we had left.

"The Finish Line is right there," she said reassuringly while pointing through a patch of trees.

"Don't lie to me, woman!" I grunted with the unmistakable sound of anger tinged with resignation.

Minutes later, we turned onto the 72nd Street Transverse. Multi-colored strobe lights flashed while the Black Eyed Peas' party anthem *I Gotta Feeling* blared from the Band Shell speakers.

Simultaneously exhausted and exhilarated, I turned to Jennifer and asked between gasps, "Are … you … happy … now?" Without missing a beat, she replied, "A real man could do that again."

And so I unwittingly began my journey toward the 2010 ING® NYC Marathon.

I LIKEN MY NEW YEAR'S EVE EPIPHANY to the New Testament account of the Pauline conversion. Saul of Tarsus was a Pharisee and understood the persecution of Christians to be his life's mission. And Saul was a man who enjoyed his work. On the road to Damascus, Saul was knocked off his donkey and onto his ass in the presence of the resurrected Christ. Literally blinded by the light, Saul was led to Ananias who laid hands up the sightless man, causing scales to fall from his eyes. Upon the restoration of his sight, Saul adopted the name Paul, became the Apostle to the Gentiles, and dedicated his life to preaching the Gospel of Jesus.

Though notably less dramatic, my embrace of the running life had a similarly profound effect on my lifestyle.

I attribute my initiation to the long-distance running community to therapy. Couples grow apart when they cease to share common interests. If the law is a jealous mistress, then running is an insatiable lover. Jennifer and I had been together more than nine years. Each of us had too much invested in our relationship to be driven apart by the friction of a unilateral obsession.

On January 23, 2010 I accepted Jennifer's invitation to attend a TFK workout in Central Park. The plan was to run a single, relaxed lap around the Jacqueline Kennedy Onassis Reservoir, a distance of slightly more than 1.5 miles.

TFK's then-head coach, Frank Handelman, is a fellow faculty member at the Fordham School of Law. A former Ohio high school standout and collegiate star at Pitt, Frank had assembled an equally-impressive coaching staff.

A few minutes after 9:00am I met Asteria Howard, who once won the Bolivian 100m National Championship while running barefoot. She later competed for both the Bolivian and Venezuelan national teams.

Asteria is a no-nonsense professional who brings the same intensity to instruction as she does to her own athleticism. Her husband, Sid Howard, is an honest-to-goodness legend who re-discovered running at age 39. Sid ran a quartet of sub-3:00:00 New York City marathons between the ages of 39-44 and holds 5 Masters age group World Records.

Asteria greeted me with her signature smile. She led the pre-run stretching exercise. Matt, Sondra, and Stephanie looked surprised to see me. I made no attempt to mask my displeasure for the endeavor. I spent the majority of the brief run complaining.

Upon finishing, Asteria came over and said she looked forward to seeing me at the next workout.

"Don't bet on that," I sniped.

Anyone who has undertaken a fitness regimen knows that the secret to success is pushing through the inevitable aches and pains that punctuate the first weeks. With grumbling assent, I committed to doing what I needed to do.

On February 20th, NYRR staged the 4-mile "Run for Haiti," a relief effort to benefit the victims of a 7.0 magnitude earthquake that claimed more than 100,000 lives and affected an estimated 3,000,000 in total. The opportunity to make a symbolic show of solidarity with those who had lost everything provided sufficient motivation to lace up my running shoes. To this day, that cotton T-shirt has great sentimental value.

A month later, Jennifer and I traveled to Salt Lake City, UT to support her *alma mater*, Butler University, in the NCAA Men's Basketball Tournament "Sweet 16." We found the "Running of the Leopards 5k," a favorable downhill course which enabled me to register my first sub-8:00 pace.

Seven days hence, we journeyed to Indianapolis, IN for the Bulldogs storied run to the National Championship Game. On the morning of the Semifinal, we drove 45 minutes to Bloomington for the Indiana University "Circle of Life Mini Marathon." This came as a surprise to me, as the longest I had ever run (and badly) was 8 miles on one occasion in 1984.

I raised this point with Jennifer. She told me not to worry. I could simply drop out if I should feel the need to do so.

Here's the thing. I am not a quitter, and she has always known that. Casting caution to the wind, we toed the line. The pace was manageable through the first 6 miles, and the thrill of competing in my first half marathon kept me distracted from the unprecedented undertaking.

At Mile 7, the skies darkened and then opened. I wondered if this was a divine omen.

As we passed the Mile 8 marker, I turned to Jennifer and said, "Well, it should be interesting to see what happens now." I grew more excited as the conditions steadily worsened.

At Mile 9, I heard Jennifer to make a statement that she today steadfastly characterizes as apocryphal. She told me, "If you can get to Mile 10, you'll definitely finish. Everybody does." Who was I to let self-doubt challenge unassailable logic?

The only significant hill appeared at Mile 11. Emboldened by the bogus can't-lose statistic, I attacked the incline. My euphoria was such that I actually ran backward for several meters until we made the crest. We raised clasped hands as we crossed the Finish Line mat in 2:06:52. The photo enjoys a place of prominence in my office.

Although I have completed more than 40 half marathons in the intervening years, that finisher's medal remains a treasure.

APRIL 10, 2010 WOULD BECOME my first – and to date only – gender-bending experience. NYRR, in partnership with *More* Magazine, annually presents the *More*/Fitness Women's Half Marathon. It is an empowering event which affords female runners the opportunity to strut their stuff during two loops of Central Park.

Jennifer registered for the race. Since we normally did our long runs together on Sundays, she suggested that I shadow her outside the cones that delineate the official course. On paper, this seemed like a good idea.

The start time weather was normal for an early spring day in New York: 47 degrees with light rain. We made it through the first 6-mile circuit at a comfortable pace. In fact, the next 7 miles were equally uneventful. But running requires situational awareness, a skill I had not yet honed.

Lost in conversation, I found myself beside Jennifer inside the shoot with no way to exit. Horrified that I had just become a "bandit," I pulled the cap down and raised my arm to obscure my face from the Finish Line photographers. And in that moment, I became the anti-Kathrine Switzer, *sans* intent or political agenda.

It remains the only time I've ever finished first in my gender division. (For the record: I did not accept a finisher's medal.)

One month later, we returned to the Hoosier State for the OneAmerica® 500 Festival Indy Mini, then the nation's largest half marathon. I finished in 1:49:16, the first time I broke the two-hour barrier.

A joy unique to the novice runner is that nearly every occasion to wear a race bib results in a personal record ("PR"). And that feeling never, ever gets old. Just ask a highly conditioned, experienced runner.

On May 16th, I accomplished another milestone, finishing 10th among the Men's 40-44 Age Group in the NYPD Memorial 5k. This was a novel validation of a worthwhile performance, and another indicator of my improving fitness.

As the calendar turned to June, Jennifer suggested that I join Team For Kids.

"Why?" I asked in puzzlement.

"To secure guaranteed entry to this year's ING Marathon," she replied nonchalantly.

This seemed absurd. Less than six months earlier, I was doubled over, grabbing my shorts for breath at the conclusion of a 4-mile fun run. Sure, I appreciated my progress. I'd come a long way in a short time. But battle what author Gail Kislevitz has aptly termed the "26.2-mile Monster" in four months' time? No way.

A week later, I wrote a $2,600 check to cover my fundraising obligation, received the distinctive lime TFK singlet, and joined a few dozen other hopeful marathoners-in-training for my first Monday night workout.

TFK is a fantastic experience. The coaches are first-rate and the training plan is aggressively tailored to the unique needs of the weekend warrior set. Most importantly, similarly situated athletes provide effective training partners and a mutual support network.

As I would come to learn, the marathon is a greater test of mental toughness than physical prowess. No one understands a rookie's phobias like those who share the struggle.

I was blessed with Sid Howard's mentoring and friendship. This man is perhaps the most unassuming, self-effacing luminary in the national running community, a characterization he roundly rejects.

The extent of our commonality appears to be as follows: we grew up in New Jersey, we each took a nearly two-decade hiatus from running, and we both enjoy the love and unwavering support of strong women.

Throughout that summer and into the early autumn, Sid inspired me by word and deed. His enthusiasm was infectious. When I began to sustain over-use injuries, he reminded me that not every run is a race, and not every race is a PR. When I was hesitant to take a day off to recover, he counseled, "Just because you can do something, doesn't mean you should."

On July 11th, Jennifer, Matt, Sondra, Steph and I competed in the 33rd Annual Utica Boilermaker, America's largest 15k road race. Aside from being the site of the National Distance Running Hall of Fame, "The Second Chance City" is Steph's hometown. Our pre-race meal consisted of local delicacy chicken riggies (chicken and rigatoni pasta, for the uniniti-ated) at local haunt Ventura's.

The on-course support was more than I had experienced in Manhattan. For more than three decades, residents of Utica's diverse neighborhoods have competed for the title of most enthusiastic booster. I was intrigued by the offering of unofficial amenities including "Kelly's Popsicle Stand."

I finished in 1:19:02 and re-joined my friends to savor post-run liquid carbs provided by local brewer Saranac and tomato pie at Steph's dad's home.

As Marathon Sunday drew closer, I enjoyed success in a pair of early autumnal half marathons.

On September 12th, I broke the 1:40:00 barrier at the Lehigh Valley Health Network VIA Half Marathon and secured Second Place in the Men's 40-44 Age Group.

On October 10th, I registered a 1:34:18 finishing time at the NYRR Staten Island Half Marathon. The performance was a PR and also earned me USA Track & Field Masters All-American honors.

NYC MARATHON WEEK BEGINS with a 5-mile race in Central Park. The 2010 event occurred on Halloween. By tradition, adventurous participants wear costumes. I donned a one-piece, poly-foam banana getup.

Want to know humiliation? Get passed by produce.

Despite the attire, I finished in 34:45, the first time I demonstrated a sub-7:00 pace. The effort also garnered my second USATF Masters All-American recognition. I could imagine no better way to conclude marathon preparation.

I had several goals for the 2010 ING NYC Marathon. The stretch goal would be to register a sub-3:20:59 time and qualify for the Boston Marathon. Based on analysis of my various performances at distances ranging from 5k to the half marathon, and taking into account the New York course difficulty, I projected a finishing time between approximately 3:15:00 and 3:25:00. Some things would need to break my way, but I was in the ballpark.

My second goal would be to run a sub-3:30:59. This was the more reasonable result.

My safety goal was simply to run the entire marathon course without walking or stopping before the Finish Line. I had trained hard and followed the coaches' protocol.

Even if I finished in 4:00:00, I would join elite company. Short of a catastrophic medical emergency, this surely would be a *fait accompli*.

Marathoners observe certain rituals in the final days before the big race. New York runners become paranoid to take the subway to work, lest someone sneeze within the confined space and spread the common cold. Pasta replaces steak as carb-loading begins midweek. Water consumption increases to ensure adequate on-course hydration. Athletes revel in the final nights of sound rest before the inevitable jitters take hold.

On Wednesday afternoon, I visited the Church of St. Paul the Apostle, my spiritual home during law school. After making a silent petition for a good race, I purchased prayer cards featuring St. Ignatius of Loyola (Founder of the Jesuit Order) and St. Christopher (Patron of Travelers). While I trusted my training, the on-course company of those spiritual figures would provide an additional insurance policy against calamity.

Hours later I participated in "Light the Night," TFK's marathon send-off workout around Central Park's Jacqueline Kennedy Onassis Reservoir. The coaching staff encouraged us to wear glowsticks to set a festive tone.

I ran with Coach Neil Fitzgerald, a world-class Masters 800m specialist. For weeks I had debated whether to raise my arms in victory for the Finish Line photo or to sprint in with whatever energy I had left.

"You've earned the right to do whatever you want," Neil advised. "Finish on your own terms."

Those words would haunt me for years to come.

ON THURSDAY, JENNIFER AND I attended the Marathon Expo at New York's Javits Convention Center. I picked up my bib and then dropped several hundred dollars in acquisition of apparel ranging from gloves to hats and jackets. I was determined to ensure that I would remember my accomplishment for years to come. Out of superstition, I did not consider wearing any of that gear before crossing the Finish Line.

A few hours later I met with Michael A. Schumacher, DPM, my podiatrist. Dr. Schumacher cares for a number of athletes ranging from amateurs to the U.S. Men's Squash Team. I had been struggling with an inflamed big toe throughout the prior week. He pronounced me fit and wished me luck on Sunday.

My next stop was an appointment with sports massage therapist extraordinaire Kim Dodd. For several years, Kim had ministered to the U.S. Open Women's Tennis Tournament competitors.

Beginning in July, she had become a valued member of "Team White." Beyond the magic she works with her hands, Kim puts my mind in a state of Zen-like peace. In those final days of pre-race anticipation, moments of serenity were priceless.

Saturday morning began with the TFK Class of 2010 ING NYC Marathon Awards Breakfast at Rosie O'Grady's. Matt Long, a New York City firefighter who had been struck by a bus and impaled upon the handle bars of his bicycle, delivered an inspirational exhortation to the assembly.

Following the meal, my training mate, Amado Diaz, and I walked several blocks to Central Park South. We determined that we should inspect the final stretch of the marathon course.

Beginning at Mile 25, we noted the terrain, especially the notorious curb cut at the entrance to Merchants Gate. We strolled past international flags that flanked the uphill path along the last 800 meters. Out of respect for tradition (or perhaps simple superstition), we stopped short of the Finish Line.

That night, Jennifer and I visited St. Paul's for the "Blessing of the Runners," a tradition in which the priest invites marathoners to the front of the altar. He then asks the congregation to join him in invoking God's blessing for a healthy, successful race.

Steph joined us for a post-Mass pasta dinner at an Italian restaurant on W. 57th Street. After the meal, we parted company and returned home to confront what every distance runner knows will be a sleepless night.

AT 2:30AM, I GREW BORED of lying in bed. I switched off the alarm and headed for the shower. Twenty minutes later, I dressed and took a final inventory.

Maui Jim® Sport polarized sunglasses? Check. Garmin Forerunner 305™ running watch? Check. GU Energy® gels? Check. ING Marathon training cap? Check. Stretch goal-and backup-plan pace wristbands? Check.

I left our apartment at 4:00am and hailed a cab for the trip to W. 52nd Street. One of the best TFK amenities is a motor coach transport to the start at Fort Wadsworth in Staten Island. In the pre-dawn darkness, a police escort replete with lights and sirens ushered the convoy through Manhattan and Brooklyn to the Verrazano-Narrows Bridge.

And there we sat in standstill traffic.

Annoyance soon gave way to anxiety, which in turn yielded to spreading panic as those of us in Wave 1 realized that our start approached imminently.

The bus finally reached its destination, and we ran to clear the security checkpoint and deposit our post-race bags with UPS® volunteers stationed within the Charity Village.

The late arrival threw a wrench into the usual pre-run routine. For months, the TFK coaching staff had stressed the importance of limbering muscles before competing. Confused, I approached Coach Fitzgerald.

"Get to the starting corral!" he barked.

"But what about the warmup?" I asked with no small measure of confusion.

"Consider the first few miles to be a 'dynamic stretch,'" Neil replied in a voice that failed to instill me with confidence.

So much for first principles.

Fear and adrenaline combine to form a powerful pre-race cocktail. There's a distinctive sense of being alone amid the throng of Starting Line competitors, a unique purpose within a collective struggle that I had not previously experienced.

Having heard the horror stories of runners relieving themselves on the Verrazano, I considered myself blessed to start on the upper deck. With less than five minutes before the start, the field began to strip, casting aside layers of "cheapie" clothing whose utility had already been realized.

NYRR President and C.E.O. Mary Wittenberg welcomed the field. New York's then-mayor, Hon. Michael R. Bloomberg, offered greetings and then lead the 10-second Final Countdown. In the next instant, members of the New York National Guard fired the canon and we stepped off as Frank Sinatra's iconic tune *New York, New York* filled the air.

The Verrazano accounts for the first two miles of the NYC Marathon course. It also presents a logistical challenge: run the bridge too slow, lose the goal pace; run the bridge too fast, empty the tank too soon.

NYPD and television crew helicopters hovered on each side of the bridge, their beating blades adding to the drama of the experience.

As I approached the down-slope, I saw the unmistakable neon green attire of a fellow TFK runner. Marathoners, particularly those new to the distance, often write their name in large letters on their shirt to elicit spectator support. My kindred spirit's name was evidently "Fr. Vincent."

I pulled even and asked if he was a Roman Catholic priest. He confirmed that he was assigned to a parish in Chicago. With no hesitation or modicum of shame, I asked if he would be willing to throw me a blessing on the go. He smiled and did so. I wished him well and we parted company.

Successful distance running requires mental discipline and a slavish obedience to routine. I knew from experience that it is imperative to maintain electrolyte balance and hydration. I had previously discovered that my system could not tolerate the Gatorade® mixture available at the fluid stations. It caused my stomach to cramp, a situation that would spell doom for my most aggressive marathon goal.

To overcome that challenge, I had determined to take a GU Energy® gel 15 minutes before the start and every 45 minutes thereafter. I would also make certain to take water at every other station: one swish to rinse my mouth, one swallow to quench my thirst.

I had developed a bad habit throughout my training that first year. Rather than keeping my head up, I focused on the ground 6' – 8' in front of me. Aside from being a safety hazard, it also meant that every run/race course had a striking sameness. Pavement has a homogeneous appearance wherever you go. And for that reason, I have precious few vivid memories of my trek through New York City's Five Boroughs.

I DO RECALL WONDERING how long Brooklyn could possibly be. The "Borough of Churches" accounts for the longest stretch of the marathon course. I felt a measure of relief upon crossing the Pulaski Bridge, the span which marks the half-way point. I compared the course clock to my Garmin and determined that I had fallen slightly off the pace I needed to achieve the improbable Boston Qualifying time. I would not let that development dampen my spirt. No matter what happened, I was going to complete my first marathon and obliterate the 4:00 mark in the process.

The spectators in Queens were enthusiastic, in stark contrast to the silence I encountered on the structure now known as the Ed Koch (nee Queensboro, nee 59th Street) Bridge.

The Mile 16 stretch is one of the few places off limits to spectators. By that point in the contest, the spastic energy and euphoria of Staten Island gives way to the solemnity of the task at hand.

I was struck by the labored breathing and rhythmic footfalls that surrounded me. As I ran down the slope, I listened intently for the much-heralded "Wall of Sound," the explosion of support from spectators lined 6-deep against the NYPD barricades.

At the beginning of Mile 17, runners need to resist the temptation to surge up Manhattan's First Avenue fueled by crowd adulation. Nine miles is still a long way to go.

I don't recall much from the first Manhattan segment, other than the anticipation of seeing my brothers, Mike and Keith, who were waiting in The Bronx just over the Willis Avenue Bridge. Eight years my junior and identical twins, their high school team earned New Jersey State Champion cross country honors. Unquestionably, they have the running talent in the family. Either of them can pop off competitive times after extended periods of inactivity. Where my athletic accomplishments are the result of drive, theirs are born of natural ability.

Throughout the preceding 10 months, they thought I was crazy. Why would I want to run a marathon? What did I have to prove? To whom did I need to prove it? Though initially skeptical of my training, they were impressed with my improving times and race results. Ultimately, I piqued their interest in returning to the sport.

Marathoners talk of an oft-seen spectator sign at or about Mile 20 that reads, "Welcome to The Bronx. There is No Wall."

My friends, I promise you there is most assuredly a wall. The insidious nature of that obstacle is that you can't locate it on any map or take comfort when you believe you've safely navigated around or beyond it. It's there. A moving pitfall, waiting with the patience of death to violently make your acquaintance.

SPORTS NUTRITIONISTS EXPLAIN THE PHENOMENON by noting that the average person stores approximately 2,000 calories on a given day. Assuming a standard burn rate of 100 calories per mile, a marathoner will exhaust that reserve at or about Mile 20. Thus, it is imperative to consume on-course supplements of glycogen to produce the simple blood sugar glucose. Without that refueling, muscles fail to respond as they should, and bad things follow.

Even under the best of conditions, you will feel tired, and you will hurt. The little voice inside your head offers the less-than-helpful reminder that you can end the self-imposed torment at any moment, simply by slowing or even stopping.

I was determined not to succumb to the growing fatigue. As I crossed the Willis Avenue Bridge, I caught sight of my brothers. They waved a sign and shouted encouragement. Without breaking stride I moved to the right, exchanged high-fives, and picked up the pace.

Things started to change, and not for the better. I ran over the Madison Avenue Bridge and returned to Manhattan. As I passed Marcus Garvey Park in Harlem, I saw many of the young girls and boys who are beneficiaries of the TFK fund raising efforts. I wish I could say I felt a boost from their enthusiasm.

I did not.

At Mile 21 my friends, Matt and Sondra, shouted encouragement. I was beginning to have difficulty maintaining concentration. Sondra saw me well before I saw her. (I never saw Matt.) She ran alongside me for several meters and shouted out, "I love you!"

I kept going.

I continued to deteriorate both mentally and physically. Coach Asteria Howard saw me approach and grew alarmed at what she observed. She reached out as I passed, grabbed my arm, and tried to stop me. I shook her off and kept running. Asteria, not to be ignored or denied, began to run by my side. She thrust two nickel-sized glycogen tablets into my right palm.

"Take those with water!" she commanded.

I have never taken any non-prescription drugs in my life. Not once. At Mile 22, I'm pretty sure I would have gratefully accepted crystal meth from a stranger.

Bad went to worse. Marathoners are taught to run the blue line along the center of the roadway, as that mark represents the shortest distance on the course. Fidelity to the line can eliminate up to two miles of inefficiency over 26.2 miles.

By Mile 23 I knew something was going very, very wrong. To that point in the race, I had seldom strayed from the safety of the center. I began to swerve uncontrollably and was unable to hold the azure median. I found myself three or four strides to the left, then overcompensating an equal distance to the right. Several runners voiced their displeasure with my unintentionally obstructionist style as they strode past.

As an inexperienced runner, I could not understand the internal early warning. I heard people shouting encouragement from both sides of the roadway, but the sounds grew muddled. I started to feel dissociated from my body. I unsuccessfully tried to focus on the faces I passed.

I knew Coach Handelman would be waiting at the 72nd Street Transverse, and that thought provided a much-needed measure of motivation. The encounter was brief and, through no fault of his, less than satisfying. While I now recall seeing him shake his head with a smile on his face, this is likely either a recovered memory or a projection of my own disgust.

At or about Mile 24 I became completely disoriented. I have no recollection as to how I left Central Park or how I found myself on Central Park South. I cast a glance down to my Garmin. The current pace reading made no sense. I had been averaging consistently sub-8:00 miles to that point. An 11:00 pace would mean I was practically walking.

My monosyllabic, decidedly non-family-friendly exclamation perfectly captured the mix of exhaustion and frustration that permeated every fiber of my being. It was at that moment that I sensed this endeavor would not end well.

Carried forward by sheer physical memory, I struggled to place one foot in front of the other. In the next instant, my left leg went forward, and the thigh jammed as if something slammed into it. The right leg also attempted to come through and met a similar fate.

That's all I recall.

I would later learn that a photographer saw what was happening and caught me before I face-planted into the unforgiving macadam of Central Park South. That act of kindness likely saved me from a concussion or the short-term inability to eat corn on the cob.

My anonymous Good Samaritan, assisted by another kind soul (I'm told), carried me to the Medical Tent at Mile 25.5 several meters away. That's where the real drama began.

AS MY WITS RETURNED, I took stock of the situation. I didn't know where I was, but preferred not to be the human interest attraction for several thousand people.

Regardless of what race organizers would have the public believe, some spectators line a marathon course for the same reason thousands fill a NASCAR® speedway. Physical collapse adds an unrivaled human drama to what is otherwise a tedious event to observe. The Germans have a word for this phenomenon – *Shadenfreude* (the joy in another's misery).

To preserve what was left of my dignity, I asked the staffers to turn the stretcher/gurney to face away from the street. It was only much later that I realized I was not in the open but rather in a nearly fully enclosed tent. And contrary to my then-inflated sense of self, I'm now certain that I was at best a momentary distraction in an event of far greater importance.

Someone asked me for my name. I thought this was funny, as "DAVID" was conspicuously stamped across the front of my singlet in 2" letters.

My first utterance was, "Be careful with my sunglasses. They have very expensive optics!"

I'm cashed out in a tent, and my priority ran to a pair of shades. This is probably the basis for the medical team's initial impression of my "agitated" state.

I wanted to limit the impact of situation. It was bad enough that I was down and out. There was no reason to cause alarm for my family and friends who would start to wonder where I was. I needed to speak with someone who could help.

Jennifer was still on the course. I explained that my cell phone was with my bag at the TFK Cherry Hill meeting place in Central Park. I was unable to keep liquid down or to sit upright. I have no recollection of vomiting, but am told that I did.

I had a series of alarming thoughts. I knew from training that after completing a marathon, it's imperative to resist the urge to simply sit or lay down. Pushing yourself to the limit forces the body to adopt certain physiological coping mechanisms. One of those is to divert blood to active muscles, including the legs, and away from other systems (like the stomach). Once the exertion is complete, the body attempts to resume normalcy. A post-race cool-down can stave off nausea and/or vomiting caused by rapidly returning blood flow to the stomach. Continuing movement can also prevent muscle cramping.

Not only had I failed to bring about a controlled finish to my race, I had directly transitioned from upright to prone/supine.

No walking. No stretching. Nothing.

As the minutes tolled by, I anticipated the inevitable. Sure enough, my lower right calf started to cramp. The pain began to advance upward.

I remembered from high school track that the natural impulse is to fight the cramp. That's about the worst thing you can do because tension causes the spasm to spread. As beads of sweat formed on my brow and upper lip, I focused on remaining calm.

A moment later my left calf began to tighten as well. I asked the Medical Tent physician to do something. Anything.

He explained that the cramping was likely related to the condition that caused me to collapse on course. His preliminary diagnosis: hyponatremia.

During the race my fluid consumption consisted exclusively of water. The physician explained that the water had flushed all of the sodium out of my system, causing an extreme electrolyte imbalance. He described my condition as "potentially life threatening."

In retrospect, I received this news with surprising calm. My demeanor changed minutes later when I experienced tingling in my left arm from my finger tips to the elbow. This development concerned me. And judging from the look on the faces of Medical Tent staffers, I wasn't alone. To my knowledge, I had never had a heart attack. I was hoping to continue that streak.

Strange thoughts will enter your mind during crisis. In the 1985 movie *Spies Like Us*, an Afghani freedom fighter implores undercover operatives played by Dan Aykroyd and Chevy Chase to operate on his ailing son. Prior to the procedure, the tribal chieftain warns the poseur surgeons, "To die in battle is glorious. To die in a tent is disgrace."

Of all the profound, introspective wisdom I could contemplate, that chestnut stayed with me. Sadly, I couldn't agree more. If the medical staff was hamstrung in its well-intentioned ability to secure adequate emergency care, I would take my chances outside the tent.

Monday's edition of *The New York Times* would report that the medical tents and their staff were fully equipped to handle various maladies which could foreseeably befall marathoners. Dehydration is among the most common health concerns in an endurance event and is easily treated through the administration of intravenous ("I.V.") fluids. The medical staff had no means to administer I.V. But they did have defibrillators, and the volunteers had been trained to use that equipment.

As I lay on the gurney, I thought about my possible kinship with Pheidippides, the modern marathoner's progenitor. According to legend, in 490 B.C. he ran from Marathon to Athens to bring news of the Greek army's victory over the Spartans. Upon delivering the message, he is reported to have exclaimed, "*Nike! Nike! Nenikékamen!*" ("Victory! Victory! Rejoice, we conquer!") and then dropped dead from exhaustion.

For a fleeting moment, I considered grasping the doctor's hand to offer my best Hellenic harrier imitation. Realizing it might confuse the volunteers into believing I had gone into cardiac arrest, thereby causing them to hit me with the paddles, I decided to save the humor.

The Medical Team made multiple unsuccessful attempts to get an ambulance transport. They informed me that the FDNY refused to send a rig across the marathon course, despite having two sitting idle at the Finish Line Medical Tent. It soon became apparent to me that the *status quo* was not going to change, absent some affirmative act on my part.

After 45 minutes the staff made the decision to administer two restaurant take-out packets of salt, which brought me around in less than 15 minutes. Now able to stand, I decided to seize the window of opportunity.

The last recorded net time near the point of my collapse was 3:27:18. Even with the unscheduled pit stop, I would have finished in approximately 4:40. But when I attempted to rejoin the race, the Medical Tent staff told me that I would incur a lifetime ban from NYRR-sponsored events (including the 2011 ING NYC Marathon) if I attempted to cross the Finish Line after more than 20 minutes of inactivity.

Despite her protest that she needed to remain in the Medical Tent, I successfully lobbied a young female staffer to accompany me to the TFK rendezvous point at Cherry Hill. She convinced the physician to let me leave under my own steam.

I suffered the indignity of having to complete the 0.70-mile journey parallel to, but just outside, the marathon course.

Now a mere spectator, I dejectedly shuffled past the packed grandstands toward Tavern on the Green. The arms that I had so often visualized to be raised in triumph hung limp at my side. No smiling volunteer placed a Finisher's Medal around my neck. My reluctant escort secured something warm to wrap around my torso. It was not the space-age Heatsheet˚ that victoriously cloaked finishers, but rather a generic, polyester red blanket like that which you would find on a plane. (I still have it.)

Evidently, one of the Medical Tent staffers had walked around the TFK spot and asked if anyone there was related to me. Steph, one of my closest running buddies, got the update from the staffer. Jennifer, now up to speed, remarked that I looked like a ghost.

As an Irish-American, I have never sported a George Hamilton-esque perennial bronze glow or resorted to the fake bake. But "gray" was a new hue for me.

Coach Handelman expressed his surprise that I was up and about given my condition. In an attempt at gallows humor, he said I should blame the British.

Prior to the 1908 Summer Olympics, the official marathon distance was 25 miles. The course was lengthened to 26.2 miles to accommodate a finish in front of the Royal Box.

He put his arm around me and compassionately recounted his own inability to finish his first marathon.

I WOULD LOVE TO SAY this post-race pep talk made me feel better. It didn't. My focus shifted to communicating with family members who expected to join us for a celebratory dinner. I reached my brother, Keith, on his cell phone. He seemed incredulous that I could have looked so strong at Mile 20 and suffered such ignominious defeat five and a half miles later. Keith promised to contact our other brother, Mike, and our Mom, both of whom planned to surprise me at the restaurant.

Now Jennifer and I had to break the news to her parents, who were waiting back at our apartment in Battery Park City.

We made our way out of Central Park and toward the W. 72nd Street subway station. I grew nauseous standing on the platform. Our train was packed with marathoners and their supporters. It must have felt great to share in the solidarity of those who had achieved this life-altering/defining feat, to be awash in the euphoric endorphin rush of the "Runner's High."

Neither experience was mine. Waves of queasiness swept over me as I sat looking, and now feeling, like death (slightly) warmed over.

We got out at W. 4th Street and waited for our connecting train. I began to pace back and forth in an attempt to stave off the gut-emptying peristalsis. Finding no relief, I doubled over, hands on hips, and tried to locate a focal point on the ground. Jennifer, sensing a new exigency to my rapidly-degrading condition, suggested that we leave the subway and get a taxi. Slowly, I gimped up the stairs and stood in the street as she attempted to hail a cab. Not many passed, and those that did were out of service. After the eternity that was likely 10 minutes, our chariot arrived.

During the ride I searched for inspiration to rally for the meeting with Jennifer's parents. I knew they would be sympathetic. But it isn't easy to face anyone after a crushing personal defeat.

Most basically, I just didn't want to puke in front of my in-laws.

We walked into our apartment and were immediately greeted by our dogs, Katy and Hollister. I mustered whatever fortitude that remained and forced a smile to my lips. I excused myself to use our restroom. I stood on the scale and confirmed the obvious. At 4:00am I weighed 142.00lbs. Eleven hours later I registered 135.50lbs.

Weight loss is regarded as a reliable indicator of dehydration. By way of illustration, on-course loss of 3% of one's body weight is considered significant dehydration. Loss of 5% is deemed to prefigure exhaustion. Against those criteria, my 4.6% drop explained what I felt.

Our guests were gracious. They understood the need to reschedule our dinner and headed home. Jennifer, who had been counseling me to go to the hospital, put me on the phone with our cardiologist friend, Matt. Aside from being a respected medical professional, Matt also knew first-hand the insidious nature of hyponatremia. It struck him at Mile 26 in his first marathon and he had exhibited the same classic signs. He, too, had difficulty getting medical treatment after the race. And even though he is a physician, the medical staff would not run an I.V. line.

I told Matt I didn't want to go to the Emergency Room. I just wanted sleep. He plainly explained my choices: Go to the E.R., get some fluid, and feel better within an hour, or remain dangerously dehydrated and out of electrolyte balance with nausea for several days. I trust Matt implicitly and reluctantly headed to the facility today known as New York Presbyterian Lower Manhattan Hospital.

The E.R. was quiet. The attending doctor informed me that I was their first, and thus far only, marathon casualty. I later learned that this was in stark contrast to the war zone of St. Luke's-Roosevelt Hospital, the closest medical facility to the Finish Line.

The doctor informed me that my vital signs and blood test confirmed the Medical Tent physician's preliminary diagnosis of extreme hyponatremia. I also presented signs of severe muscle damage.

Evidently, my well-intended, though misplaced, attempt to properly hydrate both in the days prior to the marathon and while on course flushed nearly all of the sodium out of my body, causing a state of super-hydration and, apparently, water intoxication. Diagnostic tests revealed that my kidney function was reduced to almost nothing.

One of the nurses ran a line into my left arm and began to administer fluid.

By the time I had absorbed three-quarters of the first bag, I felt much better, just as Matt said I would. I asked the doctor when I could expect discharge. He replied, "When you can pee."

Easier said than done.

Keith met us at the hospital. By 10:30pm I was working on bag #5. I asked the nurse if I could go home. She told me that patients in my condition are usually admitted overnight. Upon my solemn promise that I would drink mass quantities of Gatorade and take it easy the next day, I was discharged shortly after 11:00pm.

Total cost of the E.R. visit: $2,565.87, a nearly dollar-for-dollar push with my $2,600.00 TFK fundraising commitment. Jennifer, Keith, and I enjoyed a late-night consolatory dinner at the Gee Whiz Diner on nearby Greenwich Street.

MY FIRST MARATHON did not end as I had hoped. But I gutted it out to the point where everything faded to black. I could have stopped, but did not. I literally ran myself into the ground.

The man I was prior to that day likely would have opted for a different course of action. I can't convey the pride I still feel for leaving it all out there. Whatever quit or mental weakness may have saddled my personality through the first 40 years of my life died on Central Park South. For that, I am eternally grateful.

In 1973, Aerosmith front man Steven Tyler opined, "You've got to lose to know how to win." I now have a richer appreciation for that perspective.

On November 7, 2010, 45,350 runners toed the line at Fort Wadsworth, and 44,829 crossed the Finish Line in Central Park 26.2 miles later. I am pleased to speculate that of the 521 who did not complete the course, I may have gone farther and grown the most. Even now I believe that what might be viewed as a spectacular failure is actually a soaring victory.

In the final analysis, I would rather DNF ("Did Not Finish") than DNS ("Did Not Start").

PART II:

The Road To Reclamation

"The marathon is a charismatic event. It has
everything. It has drama. It has competition.
It has camaraderie. It has heroism. Every jogger
can't dream of being an Olympic champion,
but he can dream of finishing a marathon."

—Fred Lebow, New York City Marathon Co-Founder

A WISE MAN ONCE OBSERVED, "If at first you don't succeed, quit. No sense in being a damned fool."

My initial attempt at the marathon ended on a down note. In less than 11 months, distance running had transformed me from being an over-weight desk jockey to a USA Track & Field Masters All-American. I credit the metamorphosis to Team for Kids ("TFK") Head Coach Frank Handelman and his staff of committed assistants. Moreover, I forged several meaningful friendships which flourish to this day.

Despite the upward trajectory of my rookie season, the event which should have been the culmination of a dedicated commitment to training resulted in ignominious defeat and short-term humiliation. A "did not finish" ("DNF") result at Mile 25.5 – so tantalizingly close to victory – was never in the cards. That was not how the story was supposed to end.

In preparation for the 2010 ING New York City Marathon, I received the "Blessing of the Runners" at the Church of St. Paul the Apostle and ran with prayer cards of devotion to St. Ignatius of Loyola and St. Christopher. I even flagged down a marathon running-priest for an on-the-go blessing on the downslope of the Verrazano-Narrows Bridge. I thought I had covered every devotional base to ensure success.

And what did those pious efforts get me?

Nothing.

Six hours in New York Presbyterian Lower Manhattan Hospital and five bags of I.V. fluid were my reward for five months of training. I felt like disillusioned Lutheran Bishop Fred Pickerling of *Caddyshack* fame who denied the existence of God after a failed bid to set the club record.

OK. I didn't become an atheist, and I didn't search for answers at the bottom of a whiskey bottle. I probably should not have invested superstitious adherence to the Roman Catholic "Little Tradition." But I felt justified anger that something so sure could have gone so wrong.

I woke on November 8th (a/k/a "Marathon Monday"), showered, dressed, and accompanied my wife, Jennifer, uptown to the Marathon Pavilion in Central Park. My name did not appear in *The New York Times* Marathon Special Section. I had no medal to engrave, no limited-edition finisher gear to acquire. That reality did not dampen my pride for Jennifer's accomplishment.

We enjoyed an early lunch at Churrascaria Plataforma, a Brazilian steakhouse in Midtown Manhattan. Several rounds of Caipirinha helped to dull my disappointment.

Upon returning home, I saw the Marathon Expo bag I had acquired the previous week. It was filled to the brim with garments I would never wear. This was the first epiphany regarding the long-term social challenges I would face beginning later that day.

I HAD SECURED GUARANTEED ENTRY to the 2010 ING NYC Marathon through Team For Kids, the official charity of the New York Road Runners. With the notable exception of the Marathon itself (a situation for which I have no one to blame but myself), my experience with TFK was uniformly positive.

Each year, TFK holds a post-Marathon get-together to celebrate its athletes' accomplishments. I struggled with the decision whether to attend. I knew it would be a room full of jubilant people, each of whom would sport their Finisher's Medal. By design, this would be the forum to exchange war stories, all but two of which would end with the inevitable recounting of the glorious approach to the Finish Line. (One other TFK-er DNF-ed within the first 10 miles. I suspected he would skip the festivities. That hunch proved to be correct.)

Embarrassment aside, there were reasons that militated in favor of attending. I was fully invested in the training program. I had proudly worn the distinctive neon-lime TFK singlet at pre-Marathon races throughout the nation, and even took several age group awards while doing so. I toed the line on Marathon Sunday and attacked the course. In fact, I arguably hit it harder than most of my contemporaries, since I ran to the point of unconsciousness. The problem was that the course hit back with a 12th Round haymaker knockout.

I decided to put on my brave face and bring proper closure to the experience.

The scene at The Parlour on W. 86th Street was as I had expected. And why shouldn't it have been?

In January 2013, United Kingdom publication *The Daily Mail* conducted a survey of the top 50 bucket list adventures. Running a marathon came in at #43. It's an incredible accomplishment. While I in no way felt kinship with the revelers, I was determined not to be Debbie Downer at their event.

I worked the room and offered thanks to the coaching staff. To my self-absorbed surprise, it turned out that none of my team mates were aware of my failure. They simply assumed that I, like they, had achieved what we had set out to do. It was, after all, a logical assumption. We were runners. I had done the weekly workouts. I had completed the 20-mile weekend long runs. I had trained with the fastest group of TFK's New York novices. Most importantly, I was in the room.

I stayed for Coach Handleman's final reflection and toast, then exited with the "Irish Goodbye," apropos of the venue.

This had been the easy part. I dreaded the more socially awkward encounters to come.

EVEN THOUGH I SELF-SPONSORED the $2,600.00 TFK fund-raising commitment, that did not mean I trained in anonymity. For five months, family members and friends tracked my progress and voiced their encouragement. It would have been delusional to believe that they would not inquire about my finishing time. And that stressed me out in a way my Medical Tent and hospital E.R. travails had not.

I majored in Philosophy for several reasons. I place a premium on living by a moral code. As a practicing attorney, my professional activities are governed by a formalized canon of ethics. Primary among those tenets is the obligation for truth telling. This forced me to think (and overthink) the classic esoteric question: what is truth? On a related note, to whom do I owe a duty of candor?

When a non-runner asks, "Have you ever run a marathon?" what they really mean is, "Have you ever *completed* a marathon?" The question invites a certain moral peril in the reply, because seasoned competitors understand what the other party really wants to know.

Ethicists generally agree that a lie is an intentional distortion of facts designed to produce deception. A more granular analysis reveals that lies can be statements of commission (what you say) or omission (what you withhold).

Intellectual honesty aside, social convention favors straight talk. The law school students who I taught, fellow faculty members, and those with whom I had trained would reasonably inquire about my result. These were not people looking to revel in my failure. They simply wanted to know about my grand adventure.

The wheels in my head kept turning.

In the 1990s, I served as the Communications Supervisor for United Parcel Service's Metro New Jersey operations. Being a Fortune 50 media liaison taught me a thing or two about spin doctoring. But mere days removed from public humiliation, the last thing I wanted to do was engage in personal crisis management.

To further complicate matters, I possess an extraordinarily common name. Even the use of my middle name (Michael) does little to distinguish me from my eponymous peers. I don't need the federal witness protection program to hide in plain sight. This often works to my advantage.

Sometimes, though, it does not.

There was a gifted athlete, 16 years my junior, who resided in Manhattan. He consistently demonstrated times of which I was envious. As fate would have it, that David White was among the 2010 ING NYC Marathon field. So, too, was a pair of other "David Whites": a 41-year old from Canada, and a 57-year old from the state of Washington.

Hell, for all I know there could have been more. This was simply the trio who finished.

It's difficult to remain secretive in the Information Age. One of the race amenities for marathoners is the Athlete Tracker. Today, supporters receive real-time progress updates via a smartphone app. In 2010, a delayed system of text message alerts conveyed on-course progress. Spectators received notice of mile-, 5 kilometer-increment, and 13.1-mile progress.

I was on pace to accomplish something special for a novice marathoner. Although my hope to achieve the coveted Boston Marathon qualifying time was realistically dashed by the time I crossed the Pulaski Bridge, the effort was still impressive. It must have been utterly confusing when those reports ceased at Mile 25.5.

Like a jetliner that inexplicably disappeared off the radar, I simply vanished.

For many who cared, the logical explanation would have been to chalk up the silence to a glitch in the software. But we live in an era of social media stalking. A motivational sign I once saw read, "Pain is temporary. Internet times are forever." And yet in my circumstance, there was no record of the performance.

Most non-runners assume they could never complete a marathon. Paradoxically, those same doubters assume that everyone who toes the line will finish the race. It was therefore understandable that the inquiring minds who sought to speak with me drew the presumption that I had achieved my goal.

I let the messages in my email inbox pile without reply, and the voice mails on my phone go unreturned.

The in-person well-wishers were harder to duck.

"How'd it go?" they asked.

"I was pleased with the effort," I sidestepped.

"What was your time?" This required a more Jesuitical response.

"I went through Mile 25.5 in 3:27:18," I said confidently.

Amazingly, I don't recall anyone pose the obvious follow up: "Right. But what was your finishing time?"

Undeterred, I reluctantly continued my campaign of avoidance and obfuscation throughout that week.

In 1969, American psychiatrist Elisabeth Kubler-Ross authored the seminal work *On Death and Dying*. She theorized that those who face their own impending death or encounter the loss of a loved one experience the "Five Stages of Grief": denial, anger, bargaining, depression and acceptance. With slightly less melodrama, I gauged my own progress against that surprisingly accurate continuum.

Three weeks after the marathon, I drafted a long-overdue reply to Ian Mackler, Esq. He and his attorney wife, Debra Wolf, became two of the discrete number of friends with whom I shared my vulnerability. Both are fellow faculty members at the Fordham University School of Law.

In 1991, at the age of 49, Ian completed the NYC Marathon. I felt confident he would consider without judgment. That missive was the genesis of this work.

Ever the *mensch*, Ian sagely offered the most consoling perspective I could have received.

In June 1950, French mountaineer Maurice Herzog led the first team to summit a Himalayan peak over 8,000 meters. Triumph soon turned to tragedy as the two-week descent was marred by exposure-induced frostbite. A physician performed emergency field amputations caused by gangrene. Two of Herzog's companions lost all of their toes, while he suffered the loss of most of his fingers.

Herzog chronicled the account in an international best-selling book. The work concludes as follows: "There are other Annapurnas in the lives of men."

Although I was still a mess, those words more than any others helped me to regain perspective and to establish new priorities. The first of those was to finish a marathon.

Prior to competing in the ING NYC Marathon, I entertained the prospect of attaining a Boston Marathon qualifying time. Because experienced runners estimate New York City's course to be an average of 10 minutes slower than most other routes, I had the foresight to devise a backup plan.

The 2010 Zappos.com® Las Vegas Rock 'n' Roll Marathon® was scheduled for December 5th. Race organizers billed the course as fast and flat. One month removed from my first encounter with running's defining event, I reasoned that I would retain my hard-acquired conditioning and recover from the foreseeable micro-fissures and assorted ailments that usually follow the effort.

What I could not have envisioned was the failure I encountered in the final 0.70 mile. Where Las Vegas was once intended to be an enjoyable event, it soon assumed new importance. Sin City would be my shot at redemption.

On Sunday, November 14th at 7:00pm I set out for a relaxed 5 miles. It was my first post-ING NYC Marathon run. Nothing hurt. Having taken a week off, I planned to resume earnest preparation for Vegas.

I went to sleep at about 11:00pm. An hour later, I turned in the bed. As the sheet grazed my left knee, I experienced an acute, shooting pain the likes of which I had never known. Bewildered, I sat bolt upright and tried to make sense of what was happening. I eventually managed to return to sleep.

In the morning, I gingerly swung my left leg over the side of the bed. The pain returned the instant I stood. This was not good.

I decided to see if the condition would improve with the passage of a day or two. It did not.

On Thursday, November 18th I met with Alan B. Kadet, MD, my primary care physician. I brought the hospital diagnostic results for inclusion in my permanent file and briefly recounted the marathon failure.

Before I could explain the more recent malady, he said, "So, you're here about the heart attack."

I looked at him quizzically. Dr. Kadet stated that the blood work and accompanying tests revealed a high level of enzyme markers that would be consistent with someone who had suffered a heart attack. Fortunately, those same results are consistent with someone who has just subjected their body to the extreme physical rigor of a marathon.

I construed the ambiguity in my favor and refocused Dr. Kadet on the current ailment.

A former runner who has battled his own sports injuries, he performed a preliminary examination and expedited a referral to an orthopedist.

On Friday, November 19th I submitted to the specialist's examination. Upon learning my age (40), he smiled and informed me that running is "a young man's sport." I would do well to transition to cycling, a competitive exercise more suited to my advanced station in life.

He opined that the knee injury would heal itself with rest. To that end, he advised me to "shut it down completely" for a month and then re-assess.

I protested that I was registered for the Las Vegas Marathon in two weeks. He laughed and dismissed that scenario. Crestfallen, I asked him to reconsider the possibility. He arranged for me to have a magnetic resonance imaging ("MRI") test at 5:00pm that same day.

On Tuesday, November 23rd I returned to the orthopedist's office to review the MRI results. The doctor diagnosed a fluid-filled bulge known as a "Baker's cyst" behind my left knee. He attributed the injury to overuse during the marathon training period.

I again inquired about Vegas. He told me it would be unlikely that I would hold up over 26.2 miles. Even if I could, he pessimistically predicted that there would be no way to achieve the time I would need to qualify for the Boston Marathon.

"Well, what about the Half Marathon?" I asked.

I already had non-refundable investments in race registration, airfare, and hotel accommodations.

"It would not be a good idea," he deadpanned.

"Will I do permanent damage if I compete in the Half?" I persisted.

"No, but you will extend the rehab period by several months," he concluded.

Dejected, I left his office and considered my options.

ON FRIDAY, DECEMBER 3rd Jennifer and I flew to Las Vegas. During the flight, I had resolved to abstain from any participation, per doctor's orders. The next afternoon, we went to the Marathon Health & Fitness Expo with our friends Matt & Sondra Martinez and Stephanie Pianka.

Competitors built to a pre-race frenzy. Vendors hawked everything from the latest shoes to nutritional supplements to post-race memento displays. Olympic Marathon Champion Frank Shorter and ultramarathon great Scott Jurek shared their tips for success.

I walked inside, absorbed those stimuli for about a minute, and then headed to the registration booth. The staffer told me that I could switch from the Full Marathon to the Half if I so chose.

Hhhmmm …

What's the harm, I reasoned? I'll just pick up the race packet for which I had paid.

Jennifer looked at me with suspicion and asked, "Why do you have that?"

I replied, "I'm just preserving options." We continued to mill about the aisles.

A glassware display stood near the exit. I beheld a pint glass decorated with the Rock 'n' Roll® Series logo, a casino chip, and the event date. I picked it up and considered the situation. That was the moment I cast caution to the wind.

I turned to Matt, a pediatric cardiologist who has often graciously served as my running medical consultant, and asked what I should do.

"Go for it!" he smiled.

And I did.

UNLIKE TODAY'S FORMAT, the 2010 race started at 7:00am. It remains the only day of the year that city officials close The Strip to vehicular traffic.

Sondra hoped to break 1:54:00, a mark which was then her half marathon personal record ("PR"). Prior to my injury, I had consistently demonstrated times in the 1:30s. But I had not run a step in 3 weeks per my orthopedist's "complete shutdown" strategy.

As we stood at the Starting Line, I turned to her and remarked, "I don't know what I have today, but I'll give you what I've got."

The horn sounded, and we were off. Less than a quarter mile in, it felt like someone had jacked an ice pick under my left kneecap. The reality of what I was about to encounter for the next 2 hours became immediately clear.

To compensate for the pain, I adjusted my gait. This was precisely what the specialist told me would happen. It was also the action that would inflict further damage to my already-compromised knee.

With every excruciating step, I could feel my rehab period lengthen.

At Mile 2, I fell in behind a woman whose shirt was emblazoned with the United States Marine Corps logo. The words beneath read, "It Could Always Suck Worse."

Maybe.

Las Vegas is the home of the double-down. If I was going to knowingly injure myself, then by God it was not going to be in vain. I was all in on Sondra's quest for a PR.

We established and maintained a solid pace throughout the majority of the race. As so often happens, life got tough in the later miles.

By nature, I am a raconteur. Under stressful conditions, I do not shut up. I regaled Sondra with anything that came to mind.

I continuously consulted my Garmin running watch. If we achieved the goal, it would be by the slimmest of margins.

My words of positive encouragement took on an urgent tone. As we approached the final mile, my exhortations grew manic.

In the final stretch, I turned to Sondra and started screaming at her to finish strong. (The official Finish Line video captures the visual but not the audio effect.) We crossed in 1:53:25 and realized Sondra's goal.

Victory was ours.

We waited for Jennifer, Matt, and Steph to finish. Within 15 minutes, my left knee locked. Time to pay the piper.

To this day, I don't regret the decision for a moment.

We saw marathon champion Meb Keflezighi dressed in jeans standing alone at a table in the parking lot. Meb was selling his newly released book, *Run to Overcome*. One of our sport's goodwill ambassadors, he greeted us with his ubiquitous smile and chatted for a moment. I then gimped to the race-day merchandise stand and purchased a finisher tech shirt. This was one of two souvenirs I would treasure. The other is the fateful Expo pint glass that I continue to use.

The five of us had reason to celebrate. We returned to the hotel, showered and headed to the poolside bar.

You know what's not a good thing to do when you've just run a half marathon on an already-inflamed knee? Hot tubbing.

Hey, you live and you learn.

On December 8th, we boarded the return flight to New York. I took the aisle seat in the event I would be unable to straighten my leg after a 6-hour flight.

Two days later, I returned to the orthopedist. The examination confirmed his prior prediction. I had made my decision, and now I had to live with the consequence of that choice.

ON DECEMBER 14th, I BEGAN MY REHAB at Finish Line Physical Therapy. Owner and therapist Michael Conlon is a veteran of 25 marathons and 3 Ironman® Triathlons. His professional competence is rivaled only by his affable nature. Michael and I would get to know each other all too well over the ensuing 3 months.

I chose Finish Line as my PT provider because of their reputation for innovative care. At the time, they were one of 3 locations in New York to utilize the state-of-the-art Alter-G® Anti-Gravity Treadmill®.

Designed with input from orthopedic surgery pioneer Dr. James Andrews and marathon champion Alberto Salazar, the Alter-G operates with a combination of wetsuit-like shorts and an inflatable compartment that surrounds the user from the waist down. The machine can simulate an up to 80% decrease in body weight to drastically reduce impact on injured parts.

Despite commendable efforts by Michael and his therapist colleague, Danielle Sabella, my progress was slow going. With the exception of the New Year's Emerald Nuts Midnight Run, I had not run a mile in all of

January. By February, I had lost most of my hard-earned conditioning and grew restless. Something had to change.

On February 7th, I spoke with James J. Kinderknecht, MD, one of the nation's leading sports medicine physicians. He invited me to see him at Manhattan's Hospital for Special Surgery ("HSS"). Four days later, I met the man who I chiefly credit for getting me back on my feet.

Dr. Kinderknecht is an individual whose intensity is first evident in his eyes. He is a native Midwesterner with "Show Me State" values and has served as team orthopedist for the University of Missouri, the New York Football Giants, and the New York Mets. While I was initially impressed by his curriculum vitae and HSS's reputation as the premier health care facility for my type of injury, it was Jim's candor that earned my trust.

"You can rest that knee till you're dead, but that won't fix the problem," he flatly opined.

He advised that I undergo a second MRI, this one to be administered at HSS.

"In most places, the technicians are radiologists," he explained. "Here, these folks are physicists who utilize the equipment they innovated."

I was sold.

Upon receiving the results, I returned to Dr. Kinderknecht's office. He rotated the 3D images to show me the extent of the damage and identified a trio of problems: (1) the Baker's cyst; (2) patellar tendonitis; and (3) hamstring tendonitis, all localized in and around my left knee. We had defined the scope of the problem.

"I'll let you run with pain, but not if it risks further injury." From that point forward if he said "jump" I asked "how high."

I teach the *Advanced Client Counseling Seminar* at Fordham Law. I am well-versed in the tension between paternalism and client (patient) autonomy.

Did I want a measure of self-determination in my treatment? Not really. What I wanted was a result.

Based on my research, Dr. Kinderknecht was best suited to address my injury. He could have had zero bedside manner and I would have unflinchingly accepted his counsel. The fact that he is a renowned sports medicine physician and a better man is simply a bonus.

Bolstered by this new guidance, I introduced light running to my concurrent physical therapy.

It hurt. A lot.

But I was back.

WHILE THE INFLAMMATION DID LESSEN, it did not disappear. On April 7th, Dr. Kinderknecht administered a steroidal injection at the injury site. (Our recollections regarding the size and gauge of the hypodermic needle vary dramatically.) Within minutes of getting off the examination table, I felt remarkably better.

On May 15th, Jennifer and I accompanied Matt, Sondra, and Stephanie to Stroudsburg, PA for the "Run for the Red" Marathon and 5k. Jim's prescribed mileage protocol permitted me to run the 5k with Jennifer at a relaxed pace, which we did. The plan was then to cheer our friends at Mile 21.

That was the plan.

Sondra struggled with the late-mile hills for which that course is known.

"Run with me!" she implored.

What were we to do?

Jennifer joined us for the next 3 miles. I stayed with Sondra to the bitter end. Eight miles had definitely not been in the cards that morning. But the day provided yet another opportunity to demonstrate commitment to the highest ideals of our sport: camaraderie, loyalty, and the shared sense of struggle in pursuit of a goal.

I dialed back the miles for the next week and demonstrated renewed fidelity to Dr. Kinderknecht's counsel.

I sat out the NYRR Brooklyn Half Marathon on May 21st, but used the next day's "NYPD Memorial 5k" as a test of my improving fitness. The following weekend, I traveled to The Bronx to embrace the challenge of Van Cortlandt Park, a nationally renowned course about which it's been said, "You haven't lived until you've died in those hills."

On June 15th, Jennifer and I were 2 of the 89 runners who competed in the first orchestrated NYCRUNS event, "The Lousy T-Shirt Race" 5k. Today, that organization is one of the largest race management companies in the nation. We both finished in the Top 10 of our respective age groups.

Later that month, I confronted an issue that had nagged me since the previous November: the marathon. The ING NYC Marathon had exacted a heavy physical toll on my body. But the psychic damage was massive and longer-lasting.

The event is on many people's bucket list. That beast almost put *me* on the bucket list. I really wasn't sure I wanted to court calamity again.

I had secured guaranteed entry to the 2011 event through the "9+1 Program" (competing in 9 New York Road Runners qualifying races during 2010 and rendering volunteer service).

I tried to reconcile conflicting advice from two of the most influential people in my life. Sid Howard opined, "Just because you *can* do something, doesn't mean you *should* do something." In stark contrast, Jennifer encouraged me to seek closure by running the race I should have finished in 2010.

Several months earlier I had joined Jennifer, Sondra, and Steph as a member of the New York Flyers, one of New York's largest running clubs. In the Flyers I found structure within which to train and compete. It was through that system that I met two coaches who would figure prominently in my quest to achieve success.

The Flyers engaged Todd Weisse as Head Coach of the Marathon Training Program ("MTP"). He serves as Columbia University's Director of Operations for the Cross Country and Track & Field programs. A soften-spoken leader, Todd is Zen-like in his outlook.

Before enrolling in the MTP, we talked about my negative experience and going-forward concerns. I was candid with Todd in a way that does not come naturally to me.

In a nutshell, I was scared. What if my knee could not withstand the punishment of 26.2 miles? What if hydration/nutrition issues waylaid me a second time? What if I DNF-ed (again)?

More basically, what if, despite months of toil, I just wasn't good enough to equal or exceed my pre-collapse result?

Todd listened patiently. It turns out that many individuals DNF. In fact, the phenomenon is more likely to occur among elite runners than the recreational set. Seasoned athletes are mentally committed to the expenditure of red-lining exertion. Where the average competitor heeds the natural instinct to decrease effort in times of danger, a rarified few train to push through barriers of physical pain to attain their full potential.

By way of example, Todd reminded me that East African Haile Gebrselasie, who holds titles in various World Marathon Majors and with whom I shared the 2010 New York City course, had experienced a sore knee and withdrew upon crossing the Queensboro Bridge. Haile was so upset that he boarded a return flight to Ethiopia and announced his retirement from the sport. (He reconsidered that move days later.)

I consoled myself with the perspective that I was no quitter.

Unlike Haile, I had the fortitude to run until I lost consciousness. And I remained in the country.

"2011 is going to be a reclaiming for you," Todd enthused. Although he saw athletic potential, we readjusted my priorities. Step One was to help me get a marathon under my belt. Our goal was to complete, not to compete. I knew then and there that Todd was the appropriate coach for that stage of my running journey.

MTP Assistant Coach Evelyn Konrad provided the Yang to Todd's Ying. A versatile sprinter and decathlete, Evelyn would go on to earn a USA Masters Indoor National Championship and distinction as "Wall Street's Best Female Athlete."

I respected her from the first. Throughout the ensuing four months, she showed zero tolerance for my occasional pity parties. The track was a no-whine zone. "Shut up and run" succinctly summarized her approach to my training.

To be clear, Evelyn is a warm, caring person. But she understands there is a time to hold a hand, and a time to slap it. That was exactly the tough love I needed to get my head straight.

Without fail, it rained during every Wednesday speed workout. Noah never saw a weather pattern like we experienced on some of those summer nights. More than once we jokingly complained to Coach Todd that we had not signed up for the swim portion of the triathlon.

Throughout the weeks that followed, the MTP provided a structured, supportive environment in which to regain my running confidence.

Faster times evidenced improved fitness. On July 8th, Jennifer and I joined our friends for a weekend road trip to Utica, NY for the 34th Annual Boilermaker 15k. I finished in a respectable 1:14:45, a result nearly 5 minutes superior to the prior year's effort.

Three weeks later, I completed the NYRR Queens Half Marathon in 1:53:44. While nearly 20 minutes off my PR, it was my first attempt at long-course running since the struggle in Las Vegas more than seven months earlier. The performance affirmed that my knee would tolerate 13.1 miles of pounding on pavement; whether it would withstand twice that distance remained an open question.

In September, Jennifer and I ran two half marathons in the course of six days, a new feat for each of us.

We celebrated Labor Day on the pure trail course at Van Cortlandt Park. The unrelenting hills and uneven surface activated new muscle groups.

Michael Arnstein, the Fruitarian running enthusiast whose mission is to preserve running paths in The Bronx and Westchester County, was the driving force behind The Holiday Marathons. His eccentric vision was decidedly non-NYC. For each major holiday, he organized a run, rather than a race. Participants, not competitors, had the option to choose their own adventure among the 10k-ish, Half Marathon-ish, or Full Marathon-ish distances. (Neither Michael nor his kindred spirits were concerned with USA Track & Field course certifications.) You simply decided when you wanted to stop, and then banged a gong that hung beside the Finish Line.

This was running for the pure pleasure of running within a community of like-minded comrades. The egalitarian nature of those events was manifest in the bib; everyone wore the same number. For example, Labor Day's "1040" designation evoked awareness of the similarly denominated IRS tax form.

(In an unfortunate postscript, the New York City Department of Parks & Recreation refused to issue permits to The Holiday Marathons beginning in or about August 2011. This was a significant loss to those Downstate New Yorkers who pursue active lifestyles.)

On Sunday of that week, Jennifer and I traveled to "Christmas City, USA" for the Lehigh Valley Health Network VIA Half Marathon.

Bart Yasso, Chief Running Officer for *Runner's World* Magazine and the unofficial "Mayor of Running," is a native of nearby Emmaus, PA. Yasso, the event architect, remarked, "It's a course designed by a runner for a runner."

The path begins in historic Bethlehem and wends its way along a wooded path that parallels a canal. At Mile 12, the course returns to street level at the confluence of the Lehigh and Delaware Rivers and finishes on the avenue named for "The Easton Assassin," former Boxing Heavyweight World Champion Larry Holmes.

A year earlier, I took Second Place in the Men's 40-44 Age Group. In the 2011 event, I placed 10th in the same category. I felt strong and took considerable solace in the fact that I experienced no pain during or after the run. Things were looking good.

With the exception of high school and collegiate track, I had never before run a competitive distance of shorter than 5k. On September 24th, I participated in the NYRR Fifth Avenue Mile. The course begins at E. 80th Street and finishes 20 city blocks south adjacent to the famed Plaza Hotel.

Like many running events, strategy is the key to success in that race. The first 800m are uphill, while the final 600m are downhill. Sid Howard holds the distinction of being the only athlete to have competed in every staging of the Fifth Avenue Mile. He also dominates his age group and is the prohibitive favorite. When Sid talks, I listen.

He advised me to make my way to the front of the corral and hold something back during the first half. Once I crest the hill, I should let it all hang out and hold on for dear life.

The plan went awry from the inception. I was unable to elbow myself to the front and was forced to begin in the middle of the 618-runner pack. That placement caused me to weave around slower competitors in the 40-49 Age Group. I reached E. 70th Street slower than I had anticipated and turned on the jets.

One of my best on-course photos came from the second half of that race. The picture pulls in tight on my head and shoulders, while the background dissolves. A curtain of sweat slipstreams behind me to the inevitable chagrin of those in my wake. The shot perfectly captures the essence of effort.

I crossed the line in 5:53. The ability to break the 6:00-mile barrier at that point in my rehab gave me reason for optimism.

In recent years, the NYRR Staten Island Half Marathon has become the last local tune-up before the NYC Marathon. In 2010, I earned USA Track & Field Masters All-American honors by finishing the race in 1:34:18. In 2011, my goal was not to attempt a new PR, but rather to stay injury-free.

Mission accomplished.

Throughout the final weeks, Todd and Evelyn kept me focused. I had faithfully followed their training regimen. There was nothing left to do but to execute the plan.

AS MARATHON WEEK BEGAN, New York was once again in the throes of its annual love affair with distance running. The ubiquitous ING lion logo appeared on buses and billboards throughout Manhattan. Professional colleagues who normally wouldn't think to walk a flight of stairs peppered me with the usual race-related inquiries.

Question: "How long is the marathon?"

Answer: "26.2 miles."

Question: "How did you train?"

Answer: "I joined the New York Flyers and invested most weekday evenings and weekends throughout the past five months in pursuit of this goal."

Question: "Have you run a marathon before?"

Answer: <<preceded by involuntary sigh of exasperation and unconscious eye roll>> "Yes. I ran last year." (I had learned to live with the moral ambiguity.)

Question: "Why did you want to do it?"

Public Answer: "As a distance runner, the marathon is our sport's premier event. And no marathon experience compares to that of New York City."

Private Reality: I had never flamed-out so spectacularly in any aspect of my life. I needed a sense of closure, a way to prove to myself, if none other, that I could do it.

RECALLING THE LESSON OF 12 MONTHS PRIOR, I made sure to include Gatorade in my hydration effort so as not to flush all of the sodium from my system. For extra measure, I incorporated Hammer Endurolytes into my training runs. On Marathon Sunday, I would have more salt in me than Lot's Wife.

On Thursday, I visited sports massage therapist, Kim Dodd. Over the course of our 90-minute session she reassured me that I was poised for success. I left feeling relaxed in both body and mind.

That night, Jennifer and I attended the New York Flyers' pasta party. Bart Yasso was our keynote speaker. He presented an entertaining slide-show that depicted exploits throughout his life on the run. I appreciated the levity Bart brought to the evening.

On Friday, Jennifer and I went to the Marathon Expo at the Javits Convention Center to retrieve my race bib. Having run – and completed – the 2009 and 2010 ING NYC Marathons, Jennifer saw no reason to under-take that challenge. She opted to offer spectator support this time around.

We stopped by the TFK booth. A friend pulled me aside and applied a decal to my bib that would afford me access to the tent in Charity Village. That small act of kindness would spare me several hours of exposure to the wind and ground moisture. Apparently, alumni membership (or at least friendship with the right people) does have its privileges.

Mindful that I still had a shopping bag full of 2010 ING apparel that I would never wear, and a Tiffany & Co. crystal desk ornament I could never display, I was judicious in my selection of mementos. If I finished this one,

I would be first in line at Marathon Pavilion on Monday morning. While the finisher gear is limited, that merch is always more impressive.

On Saturday morning, Jennifer participated in the inaugural NYRR "Dash to the Finish Line 5k," an event through which those who do not compete in the Marathon find meaning in the weekend's festivities. The race began at the United Nations, continued past Grand Central and across 42nd Street to the Marathon Finish Line in Central Park. With the notable exception of former collegiate standouts, it is more accurately described as a "fun run" because out-of-towners stop on course to photograph the quintessential surroundings and take selfies. Those human obstacles make for a less-than-optimal environment in which to achieve a PR.

After the race, we went home and relaxed. Unlike 2010, I dispensed with the pilgrimage to the Church of St. Paul. Dinner consisted of delivery from a Battery Park City Italian restaurant. I got in bed at about 9:00pm, knowing I would get no sleep that night.

I SWITCHED OFF THE ALARM before its 4:00am setting could sound and headed to the shower.

Marathoners often write their name in large letters on the front of their singlet to elicit spectator support. For some, an enthusiastic word or two from a stranger can provide a much-needed emotional lift in the late going. I wanted no part of that. I would be just another anonymous participant among the field of 47,438 runners.

I donned my New York Flyers long-sleeve tech shirt and cap. In an intentional act of defiance, I opted to wear the tattered running shoes that had attempted the 2010 ING NYC Marathon course. I was willing to trade off shock-absorbing cushion for closure.

I kissed Jennifer good-bye and began the pre-dawn trek from our apartment to the Staten Island Ferry Terminal.

Fifteen minutes later I met Steph amid the growing throng of marathoners. We had agreed to run together.

She had done something I hadn't: finish a marathon. And not just one or two. She was a seasoned long-distance veteran who maintained a rock-steady pace.

Still battling gnawing self-doubt born of the 2010 ING NYC Marathon disaster, I was prepared to sacrifice speed for certainty. Steph would take me to – and through – the Finish Line.

We struck up a conversation with a fellow ferry passenger from Chicago. The banter helped to keep my mind off the challenge that would begin on the other side of New York Harbor. Dawn broke as we pulled into the slip at St. George. A waiting bus shuttled us to Fort Wadsworth. A volunteer scanned our bibs and we proceeded to the TFK tent where we met a number of our former teammates.

Steph collects marathon finisher Heatsheets. She withdrew two from her bag and spread them on the ground. We each consumed a banana and tried to relax. All that was left to do was to drop our bags with the UPS volunteers and begin our warm-up stretches.

I had a Wave 1 bib and opted to drop back to Wave 2 to run with Steph. We entered the holding pen and waited. At 9:40am, we heard the distant canon shot that announced the start. The 2011 ING NYC Marathon was underway. A few minutes later, our group began the slow shuffle to the Start Line.

Sondra Martinez, who completed the ING NYC Marathon in 2008 and 2009, looked at Steph and me.

"So, we're really doing this? she smiled.

"I guess so," I replied with what I hoped sounded more like cheer than doubt.

All around us, runners began to strip away layers of the disposable clothing that had provided warmth against the staging area cold. Hoodies and sweatpants flew over our heads in the general direction of the sideline.

Strangers united in the comradery of the moment offered fist-bumps and words of encouragement.

The countdown began. Sondra, Steph and I exchanged looks of reassurance.

"… 3, 2, 1!" The horn sounded, and we took our first choppy strides up the Verrazano-Narrows Bridge.

Shortly before the mid-span Mile 1 marker, Steph and I left Sondra. We had agreed to maintain a sub-9:09 per mile pace to ensure an under 4-hour finish. It would be Steph's task to keep me reigned in that day.

We came off the Verrazano and made our way toward 4th Avenue, a flat, 5-mile stretch through Brooklyn. Steph yelled "hi" to some friends who were enjoying a rooftop Marathon Sunday brunch. It occurred to me that would be a fine way to get into the spirit of things.

We turned onto Flatbush Avenue. I felt great.

"These have been the easiest 7 miles I've ever run!" I enthused.

"Easy there, cowboy," Steph cautioned. "There's a lot of road left."

Aside from the geography, she was right for reasons I did not yet appreciate.

Dr. Matt Martinez once dispensed the most succinct, useful running advice I have ever received: "Respect the distance." In the marathon, things can go badly very quickly.

We turned off Kent Avenue onto the Pulaski Bridge. As we approached the 13.1-mile mark, I felt an acute pain in my left knee.

No. NO. NO! Not a second time. Not with half the course to go.

This can't be happening.

In less than a mile my emotions ran from panic to anger. Steph saw that something was wrong. I explained the situation.

Unlike the *U.S. Soldier's Creed*, "no man left behind" is not the distance runner's pledge. The marathon is not an event that condones passive-aggressive behavior masked as kindness. Seasoned competitors know that if you run with someone, then there needs to be an express understanding that an inability to maintain the agreed-to pace is justification for the non-affected party to break away.

And there's nothing wrong with that. It's simply the operative rule of engagement. To demand anything else from a running companion reflects sheer selfishness.

A scene from the 1990 Hollywood blockbuster *The Hunt for Red October* came to me. Captain Vasili Borodin, one of the defectors on the renegade Russian submarine, lies mortally wounded in Captain Ramius's arms.

"I would like to have seen Montana," he utters, and then dies.

While I have never desired to see Big Sky Country, I did have a hankering to cross a finish line located about 12 miles from my then-current location. I turned to Steph and said, "I would have liked to have had that [celebratory] dinner."

The pain worsened. I had real concern that this would be the 2010 ING NYC Marathon, Part Deuce. I struggled for another two miles and then told Steph to leave me. Knowing that Jennifer and my brothers, Mike and Keith, would be waiting at Mile 20, I made one request.

"Tell them to go home. There'll be nothing to see," I fatalistically predicted.

And with that, Steph pulled away.

Distance running is more mental than physical. I have found the worst thing to do on a long run is to think. Unfortunately, I had about 11 more miles in which to be alone with my thoughts.

IN 2010, I LEARNED THAT MANY RUNNERS adopt a transcendental mantra during their races. The repeated recitation of a short phrase can provide the necessary inspiration to complete the task.

Although you are not likely to find me in a church pew on any given Sunday, I continue to identify with the tenets of Roman Catholicism. Theologians opine that people raise their voices to the Lord for three central reasons: (1) to give praise; (2) to offer thanks; and (3) to petition for intercession.

Running helped me to return to my religious roots. In short order, I took care of business.

I praised God for His redemptive love. I borrowed St. Ignatius Loyola's perspective and recognized myself as "a loved sinner."

I thanked God for all the great things He had brought into my life and all the truly poor things He had kept out of it.

I also asked Him to cut me a break. Like the James Taylor classic *Fire and Rain* or Carrie Underwood's contemporary country favorite *Jesus Take the Wheel*, I was convinced there was no way I would get through this ordeal without Him.

I started to recite the "Lord's Prayer" and repeated those words over, and over, and over.

I also dealt with a paradox: The harder I ran, the more my knee hurt. But the more I dialed back, the longer I would be on course, which invited a recurrence of dehydration or hyponatremia. Pick your poison.

I opted to go for broke and hammered down.

MID-SPAN ON THE ED KOCH/QUEENSBORO BRIDGE

I received a welcome surprise. I saw Steph and caught up to her. We exchanged short conversation. I told her I continued to struggle and again asked her to tell Jennifer and my brothers that I would join them at home. She agreed, and pulled away once more.

I came off the decline onto First Avenue. For the second time in as many years, I was unmoved by the "Wall of Sound." I didn't need adulation, just merciful closure.

Mike and Keith kept the faith and waited with Jennifer at Mile 17 for my presumed arrival. She chose to wear the banana outfit I had worn during the 2010 Poland Spring® Marathon Kickoff 5-miler. It made her much easier to spot among the supporters who cheered curbside. (I later learned that marathoners were applauding *her* as they passed.)

Jennifer thrust several Hammer Endurolytes and an espresso GU Gel® into my hand. I gratefully accepted them and exchanged high-fives with Mike and Keith before continuing on my way.

Three miles later, the course crossed the Willis Avenue Bridge for the one-mile detour into the South Bronx.

Veterans know the first 20 miles of the marathon are just transportation to the 10k race which separates success from failure. My knee continued to throb. The thought of grinding out another 6.2 miles was dispiriting.

I saw Sid Howard at Mile 22. The word or two he shouted to me was enough to bolster my spirits. I pressed onward.

The uphill grade on Fifth Avenue worsened an already bad situation. My legs felt like lead. I consoled myself with the thought that only a 5k stood between me and my goal. Entering Central Park at Engineers Gate was a welcome relief.

At Mile 24, TFK Coach Brian Hsia, attired as Captain America, was a real hero for one of my former teammates who had hit "The Wall." That would not be my lot. Not this year.

Minutes later I was on Central Park South. Twelve months earlier, my marathon odyssey ignominiously ended right there. Things were different this day.

As I passed Mile 25.5, I threw the finger at the Medical Tent. (I take this opportunity to publicly apologize to the confused spectators who did nothing to incur this unprovoked incivility. I like to think they would understand if they knew the backstory.)

I rounded the turn at Columbus Circle and caught my image on the Central Park video screen at Merchants Gate. I took care while entering through the narrow curb cut. A runner inexplicable stopped short in front of me. Carried forward by momentum, I put my hands forward to keep from falling.

"Come on!" I barked. I would later realize that my reaction was similar to those who criticized my obstructionist, hyponatremia-induced weaving in 2010.

With 600 meters remaining, I no longer cared about the pain radiating from my knee. I focused on completing the mission.

In races and even training runs of any distance, I always find something left in the tank for a fast finish, an ability I attribute to my experience as a high school and collegiate sprinter. I debated whether to expend the last measure of my strength to honor Pheidippides's legacy, or to strike a pose for the photographic memento of a lifetime.

As I strode up the final incline, I recalled a conversation with TFK Coach Neil Fitzgerald. A year earlier, he advised me to finish the race on my own terms. I opted for the classic arms raised in victory. If there would be another marathon, I would undoubtedly realize a faster time. If this was to be my only triumphant moment, then I would preserve it as such.

Elite marathoners take approximately 28,000 strides to cover 26.2 miles. The shorter, less efficient clip of amateur athletes dramatically increases that total. I don't have a clear recollection of any of those foot strikes, with the exception of the final step. I crossed the first of the two Finish Line timing mats, gazed heavenward, and audibly said, "Thank you."

I finished in 3:55:58, a result that continues to adorn the TIMEX® ING NYC Marathon souvenir magnet affixed to the microwave door in our apartment.

I bowed my head as a volunteer placed the coveted Finisher's Medal around my neck, while another cloaked my shoulders with a Heatsheet. I stumbled forward and accepted the post-race goodie bag. It was then that I first noticed how powerfully thirsty I was. I looked with envy upon everyone around me as they gulped from Poland Spring sport bottles. Five minutes later, I opened the drawstring bag and realized I also possessed the means to wet my whistle.

Disoriented but ambulatory was a significant improvement from my 2010 experience.

I made my way to the TFK Cherry Hill spot where I reunited with Steph. She finished exactly 2 minutes before me. We hugged and I thanked her for helping me through the first half. It is perhaps fitting that I crossed the 2011 Finish Line as I ended the 2010 event: on my own.

I found Jennifer, Mike, and Keith about an hour later. I am convinced they were more proud of me than I was of myself. And that was no mean feat.

We took the subway downtown to Battery Park City. I savored the looks of admiration from fellow straphangers. This was the experience I missed in 2010.

After showering and dressing, we dined at Churrascaria Plataforma in Tribeca. Mike and Keith, our Mom, Steph, Sondra, Matt, and Coach Evelyn joined us. This was the celebratory dinner which had been delayed 52 weeks. It was worth the wait.

NEARLY TWO MONTHS LATER, Jennifer and I took time on New Year's Eve to reflect upon our year in running. She reminded me that one of the benefits of our sport is the ability to regale others with war stories.

From her perspective, I had garnered the hat trick of archetypal tales: an uncommon athletic accomplishment (winning an age group award); a funny anecdote (setting a PR costumed as a banana); and a dramatic account (the arc that bridges the 2010 and 2011 ING NYC Marathons).

The Beastie Boys' hit *Intergalactic* intones, "I run the marathon 'til the very last mile." Whether you interpret that line to mean *until* the very last mile (2010) or *through* the very last mile (2011), I've done it both ways.

And I prefer the latter.

EPILOGUE

At Mile 20, I thought I was dead;

At Mile 22, I wished I was dead;

At Mile 24, I knew I was dead;

At Mile 26.2, I realized I had become too tough to kill.

-Anonymous

WRITING IS AN INTENSELY PERSONAL EXPERIENCE. An author consciously chooses to share private thoughts with anonymous, judgmental strangers, almost none of whom will muster the courage to expose reciprocal vulnerability.

Each of us has a unique field of experience. With that recognition, I set my shoulder to the literary plough in hope of sowing seed that would yield an anecdote that is enlightening and entertaining.

For a time, I considered "The White Marathon" (a black humor term friends coined to describe my 25.5-mile 2010 ING NYC Marathon experience) to be a badge of shame. But just as Hawthorne protagonist Hester Prynne's Scarlet Letter "A" eventually symbolized ability and self-reliance, so too did I embrace my race result.

The great myth is that completing a marathon is a life-altering accomplishment. It is not.

The priceless transformation occurs months before the starting horn sounds. It is the threshold decision to establish a long-range goal. It is the discipline to lace up your running shoes in pre-dawn chill, withering heat, or driving rain. It is the mental toughness to know that you can instantly alleviate physical pain by slowing or simply stopping, and yet summon forth the strength to place one foot in front of the other again, and again, and again.

Like Sisyphus who chose to roll the rock up the hill, the runner soldiers on not because she has to, but because she wants to.

Legendary football coach (and Fordham University alumnus) Vincent T. Lombardi once observed, "The greatest accomplishment is not never falling, but in rising again after you fall."

Life does not always unfold as we hope. We stumble. We fall.

We fail.

Sometimes, success is not immediate. For those with the perseverance to stay the course one more mile, the ultimate triumph is all the sweeter.

To all who have run – or may yet experience – their own "White Marathon," I say:

Nike! Nike! Nenikekamen! ("Victory! Victory! Rejoice, we conquer!")

New York, NY
April 2017

PHOTO SECTION

Cover Photo. Used by permission of Backprint. All rights reserved.

1. "The Future Pheidippides." My first organized distance run was the River Vale, NJ 75th Anniversary 5k (July 1981).

2. "Son, It's Called 'Hurdling,' Not 'Hurtling.'" I display the graceless form that convinced Track & Field Head Coach William D. Henshaw that I was a much better 100m, 200m specialist than a 400m Intermediate Hurdler. (He was right.)

Photo Credit: St. Joseph Regional High School (Montvale, NJ)
Aegis Yearbook, 1988. All rights reserved.

3. "A Real Man Could Do That Again." My wife, Jennifer, and I share in the revelry moments after finishing the New York Road Runners "Emerald Nuts® Midnight Run" 4-Miler in Central Park, January 1, 2010. My "runner's high" was likely the euphoria of a couch potato body successfully cashing a check written by an over-inflated ego. The struggle to complete this unscored "fun run" prompted me to lose 42lbs in less than 6 months.

4. "What Doesn't Kill You …" Jennifer and I cross the Indiana University "Circle of Life" Half Marathon finish line hand-in-hand. I had never run more than 8 miles prior to completing this 13.1-mile course on April 3, 2010.

Photo Credit: Used by permission of Hoosier Half Marathon
Race Management/INTIMECO Productions. All rights reserved.

5. "Earn Your Beer!" Utica, NY is home to the National Distance Running Hall of Fame and the Boilermaker, the largest domestic 15k field. Dr. Matt Martinez, his wife Sondra, Stephanie Pianka, Jennifer, and I imbibe the event's famous post-race amenities courtesy of the F.X. Matt Brewing Company on July 11, 2010. (l. to r. Sondra, Matt, Me, Jennifer, and Stephanie).

6. "Just a Stroll in the Park." Team For Kids Alumna (and future New York Flyers Teammate) Sondra Martinez and I knock out 18 miles in Central Park during the New York Road Runners ING® NYC Marathon "Long Training Run #1" on August 1, 2010. My wife, Jennifer, and our ever-present running buddy, Stephanie Pianka, are not far behind.

7. "Who Loves Ya, Baby?" On a rain-drenched September 12, 2010, I ran the Lehigh Valley (PA) Health Network VIA Half Marathon in honor of my beloved aunt, Jean G. Delaney, who left this world less than 48 hours earlier.

My 1:36:58 on the predominantly trail course earned Second Place in the Men's 40-44 Age Division. While I have run faster times at the distance, it remains the most emotional performance of my running career.

8. "The Top Banana." The Poland Spring® Marathon Kickoff (5-Miler) marks the beginning of the Big Apple's premier racing week. The 2010 event fell on Halloween. In the spirit of the day, I donned a three-quarter length poly-foam banana and registered a 34:45 and my second USATF Masters All-American honor.

9. "Saints Preserve Us." My 2010 Marathon Eve preparation included the "Blessing of the Marathoners" at the Roman Catholic Church of St. Paul the Apostle. The Gift Shop vends prayer cards including those which venerate Society of Jesus Founder St. Ignatius of Loyola and St. Christopher, Patron of Travelers. I tucked these into the pocket of my running shorts before heading to the ING° NYC Marathon starting line.

10. "Cold Comfort." This is the generic, nondescript blanket I received in lieu of a 2010 ING NYC Marathon finisher's Heatsheet®.

Six years later, our rescue dogs, Hollister (a former South Bronx denizen) and Katy (a Hurricane Katrina evacuee), continue to enjoy the only memento of my 25.5-mile jaunt through New York City's Five Boroughs.

11. "The Most Expensive Cocktails in Town." Post-race Emergency Room medical treatment included bloodwork and 5 bags of I.V. fluid. The bill was almost a dollar-for-dollar push with my $2,600 fundraising commitment to Team for Kids, the NYRR charity which benefits youth running.

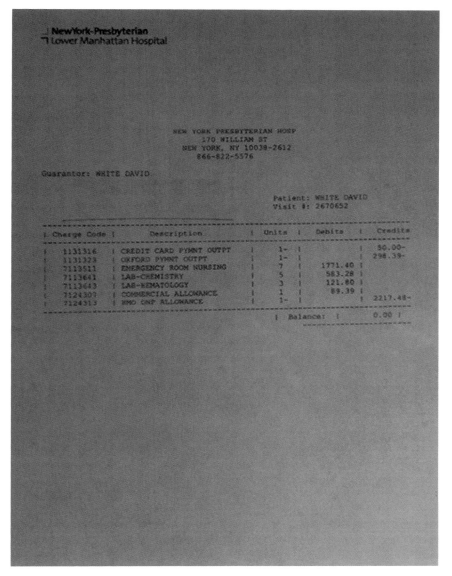

12. "Walking On Air." The Alter-G® Anti-Gravity Treadmill®, a techno-logical wonder developed in consultation with pioneering orthopedic surgeon James Andrews, MD and current Nike® Oregon Project Head Coach Alberto Salazar, enables rehabbing runners to reduce their body weight by up to 80%. Finish Line Physical Therapy, an early adopter of state-of-the-art technology, acquired one of the first two units in New York.

Owner Michael Conlon (pictured here with me) used this resource to great effect to preserve my conditioning before I was road-ready.

Photo credit: Used by permission of Adena Stevens/Studio A Images. All rights reserved.

13. "A Feast Fit for Hungry Hemerodromoi." On November 6, 2011, family and friends joined me at Churrascaria Plataforma in Tribeca for a post-ING NYC Marathon celebratory dinner that was a year in the making. As one who came to learn the uncertainty of life, I ate dessert first. (l. to r. Sondra Martinez, Stephanie Pianka, Me, and M. Murat Beyazit).

ACKNOWLEDGMENTS

This project was neither calculated to advance my professional career, nor to improve my personal finances. Of the roughly 500,000 new titles that come to market each year (half of which are self-published), only 10% sell more than 500 units. On average, authors make about $1.00 per copy sold. Cognizant of those statistics, I made the informed decision to invest hundreds of hours for a foreseeable monetary sum I could earn in a day at my private legal practice billable rate.

I wrote *Negative Splits* for one reason: to inspire those who question their ability to see a more positive tomorrow.

Richard White, a training buddy whose astounding athletic accomplishments leave us little in common save a shared surname, offers the correct orientation to completing a marathon. He opines that while each of us crosses the Finish Line under our own steam, none of us makes the journey alone.

There are many to whom I owe debts of gratitude.

The litany begins first and foremost with my wife, Jennifer L. White. Every day, in every way, she is my inspiration. "Thank you" is an utterly inadequate expression to encapsulate what she means to me. Fortunately, she knows this.

My athletically gifted brothers, Keith and Michael, provide unflagging support. They are blessed to possess God-given talent I attempt to equal through determination. While they may at times question their older brother's sanity, they should never doubt his love.

Coach William D. Henshaw opened my eyes to the wonder of Cross Country at a time when I thought 2.5 miles was "long distance," a fact I recall in the homestretch of every 5k. At the conclusion of his tenure as Head Coach of the St. Joseph Regional High School (Montvale, NJ) Cross County/Indoor/Outdoor Track & Field programs, my fellow seniors and I recognized his years of service. We presented a commemorative plaque inscribed with these words: "It's Hard to Be a Good Coach; It's Harder to Be a Good Friend. You Were Both." Nearly 30 years later, I affirm that assessment.

SJR teammates Brian Biegel, John Cunningham, Rich Harrington, John Hannan, and Clifford Jean-Louis were important influences during my high school experience.

I honor the memory of our Green Knights teammate Robert G. McCarthy, a talented 110m high hurdler, who was among the 2,606 innocents murdered at the World Trade Center on September 11, 2001.

In a fortuitous accident of history, I was a member of the Fordham University Men's Track & Field Team at one of its shining moments. Lascelles "Wayne" Seaton, Mike Scott, Steve Sharpe, and Ricky Jones, gifted sprinters one and all, taught me what it means to be a NCAA Division I athlete. My time under their tutelage was brief but unforgettable.

The 2010 New York Road Runners Team for Kids ("TFK") coaching staff enabled me to experience the joy of distance running. I whole-heartedly recommend the TFK program to those for whom running a marathon is a "bucket list" aspiration.

Former TFK Head Coach Frank Handelman is among the most knowledgeable running professionals on the scene. Assistant coaches Vincent "Skinny Vinny" Corso, Neil Fitzgerald, Brian Hsia, and Glen Wiener inspired our crew in word and deed.

TFK teammates Anthony Bonamassa and Amado Diaz provided daily motivation and much-needed good humor mile after mile during our five months of training for the 2010 ING NYC Marathon.

New York Road Runners TFK liaison Rudi Klein embodied the spirit of the program. A self-described "finisher," Rudi grinds out miles with unflinching Teutonic resolve. *Danke mein Freund.*

James J. Kinderknecht, MD of the Hospital for Special Surgery (New York, NY) is a consummate professional. Formerly a team physician for the University of Missouri and currently on the staff of the New York Football Giants and the New York Mets, Dr. Kinderknecht is a nationally renowned health care professional and gifted teacher. Whether you are an injured elite athlete or a weekend warrior on the mend, he is the man to see when you need coordinated care. Jennifer and I are blessed to count Jim and his wife, Linda, among our family's friends.

Michael Conlon, Owner of Finish Line Physical Therapy, was integral to my successful rehabilitation following the 2010 ING NYC Marathon. It meant a great deal for me to perform PT under the watchful instruction of a fellow endurance athlete. His treatment centers are state-of-the-art.

I extend special appreciation to former Finish Line Physical Therapist Danielle Sabella for demonstrating Job-like patience as I struggled to learn the (sometimes painful) craft of foam rolling.

The New York Flyers are an exceptional group of runners whose membership spans the continuum of ability. They train hard, compete with determination, and celebrate personal records with unrivaled gusto. Former teammates Ed Altman, David Gaines, Alan Gardner, Adam Marsh, Claudia Osmar, and Julie White remain friends.

I thank New York Flyers Marathon Training Program ("MTP") Head Coach Todd Weisse for being the Zen Master on my 2011 road to reclamation. His holistic approach resonated with me when I needed it most. *Namaste.*

MTP Assistant Coach Evelyn Konrad was a benevolent task mistress. The 2013 Royal Bank of Canada Decathlon Women's Champion, she earned the title "Wall Street's Best Athlete." (She should have earned combat pay for putting up with me.)

Kim Dodd, masseuse to the U.S. Open Women's Tennis Championships, time and again kneaded my sore limbs and inflamed tendons through the growing pains which accompany the transition to distance running. Her hands have been touched by God.

Michael A. Schumacher, DPM, former Chair of the United States Squash Racquets Association, literally kept me on my feet 48 hours before 2010 Marathon Sunday. Two days after the 2011 race, he drilled my left big toe to release blood that had pooled due to the trauma of an irregular foot strike. Toenails are indeed over-rated.

Fellow Fordham Law faculty members Debra J. Wolf, Esq. and Ian Mackler, Esq. are among my most steadfast friends. Ian, who successfully completed the 1991 NYC Marathon, was the first non-family member with whom I shared my 2010 ING NYC disappointment. He listened without judgment and provided a healthy perspective which turned failure to triumph. Ian's compassionate counsel inspired me to pen this highly personal memoir. *L'Chaim!*

Urban Athletics ("UA") Coach Jim Saint-Amour worked with me after the 2011 ING NYC Marathon. Under his skillful tutelage, 2012 became a year to remember as I PR-ed at the mile, 5k, 4-mile, 10k, and marathon distances. (I chronicle those exploits in the forthcoming *Negative Splits* sequel, *Beyond the First Finish Line*.)

UA training buddies Chris Faris, Jordan Kurzweil, and Joe Tracy pushed me during our pre-dawn speed and form sessions. I thank them for providing motivation during ladder workouts and Yasso 800s in Battery Park. Remember: we are each someone's rabbit.

I credit UCAN™ Registered Dietitian/Nutritionist Seth Bronheim with revolutionizing my approach to training and race-day nutrition. I was an early adopter of the miraculous, stimulant-free SuperStarch nutritional supplement. Without risk of hyperbole or prospect of remuneration, I attest that UCAN fueled my transition from decent competitor to USATF Masters All-American.

My wife, Jennifer, and I are proud to be members of Front Runners New York ("FRNY"), the Big Apple's LGBTQ running club. It is our belief that at the time we joined, we were the only straight couple among the approximate 700 members.

Our decision to join FRNY was not informed by a desire to make a radical social or political statement. We simply wanted to train with the most committed athletes in town.

The affiliation has opened our eyes to the shameful discrimination which surprisingly lingers in one of the nation's most inclusive metropolises.

Think I'm off base? I'll lend you my FRNY racing singlet. Once you experience the weight of surprisingly frequent judgmental stares and occasional homophobic innuendo, let's talk.

I fervently hope that in the wake of United States Supreme Court jurisprudence and nationwide legislative referenda, our fellow citizens will soon embrace equality for all.

FRNY Head Coach Mike Keohane, a 2:16 marathoner and Silver Medalist at the 2000 Sydney Paralympic Games, is a world-class instructor. Jennifer and I extend special appreciation to teammates Fernando Aguilar, Katrina Amaro, Tara Amato, Brenton Bellamy, Michael Benjamin, Brittany Bello, Alan Brown, Stacey Cooper, Jill Crouther, Ekong Ekong, Bernd Erpenbeck, Connor Essick, Dan Ferguson, Matt Frank, Gilbert Gaona, Elke Gasselseder, Steven Gross, Tim Guscott, Edward Kennelly, Sam Lafata, Kent Lau, Chen Liang, David Lin, Myles Lock, Diane Lowy, Mike Markowitz, Jesus Martinez, Mark Mascolini, Michelle Mazzara, Martin McElhiney, Dennis Ng, Michael Orzechowski, Paul Racine, Samecia Sanders, Maarten Vandersman, Luc Berger-Vergiat, Steven Waldon, Gen Watanabe, Richard White, Maria Woehr, and Yoshie Yabu.

A pair of Southern Connecticut State University professionals painstakingly searched haystacks for needles. I am indebted to Owls Men's Cross Country/Track & Field Head Coach John Wallin and Chief of Police/Director of Public Safety Joseph Dooley.

Sarah L. Jones deftly navigated a labyrinth of Intellectual Property matters and secured the various permissions to quote copyrighted material.

Victoria M. Vitarelli is the detailed-oriented professional to whom I entrusted the final edit of this work. I can offer no greater endorsement of her extraordinary talent.

Alan Radom of Artisan Photo Productions, Inc. lent a discerning eye to the selection of images which enliven the narrative.

Nadine Gilden of Curious Light designed the cover which graces this work and created its web presence (www.negativesplitsbook.com). Her effort provided your first impression of my labor of love.

Joe Ziemer facilitated my introduction to Nadine, a connection for which I am most grateful.

Chris Lee and W. Scott Owens provided insightful pre-publication feedback.

Maurice Q. Robinson, Esq. helped formulate a coordinated social media campaign to make the *Negative Splits* brand accessible to a wider audience.

BookBaby Product Specialist Karen Maneely and Publishing Specialist Colleen Kelley adroitly managed the publication process. They are blessings to this novice author.

Once and (I remain guardedly optimistic) future Butler University development officer Colin Brown rendered assistance from the Hoosier State.

Celebrated authors Patricia Nell Warren and Gail Kislevitz were the first to offer formal praise for *Negative Splits*. Through their respective work, each has made the sport of distance running more familiar to the public. Their endorsement of my debut publication fills me with a deep sense of satisfaction.

In 1967, "K.V." Switzer donned race bib 261 and became the first female to officially compete in the Boston Marathon. Seven years later, she was the NYC Marathon Women's Champion. In 2017, Kathrine triumphantly returned to Heartbreak Hill and distance running's defining course. Her 261° Fearless Foundation empowers and inspires women to overcome barriers to success. We stand in solidarity.

On a sunny Sunday in September 1970, Gary Muhrcke registered for the inaugural NYC Marathon 15 minutes before the starter's gun sounded. Amid unseasonal 85-degree heat and high humidity, he toed the line alongside 126 other intrepid pioneers, unaware of the historic nature of the endeavor. He was the first to break the tape (2:31:39), thereby securing his place in United States marathon lore. I am honored that Gary chose to lend his name to my writing.

Ultramarathon phenom and *New York Times* best-selling author Dean Karnazes, whom *Time* magazine named one of the "100 Most Influential People in the World" and *Men's Health* magazine honored as one of the "100 Fittest Men of All Time," recognized the merit of this project. Dean encouraged me to bring my message to market. In 2016, he penned a riveting investigative assessment of Pheidippides' real run. *The Road to Sparta: Reliving the Ancient Battle and Epic Run that Inspired the World's Greatest Footrace* is a page-turning must-read.

I am delighted to support Dean's 501(c)(3) foundation, KARNO Kids, and its mission to improve the health and wellness of our youth.

Throughout the past seven years, Matthew N. Martinez, MD has served as my unofficial on-course physician. Dr. Martinez, a noted Manhattan-based pediatric cardiologist, is an accomplished endurance athlete. It was he who convinced me to seek immediate medical treatment following the 2010 ING NYC Marathon. (It turns out, life *does* go better with I.V. fluids.) Matt remains a trusted friend and valued confidant.

Sondra Martinez, Matt's wife, is a kindred spirit. A kind, caring individual, Sondra is possibly the only competitor I know who is more intense than me on – or off – the race course. (I mean that as high praise.)

Stephanie Pianka evinces stoic discipline and a mental toughness that would make G. Gordon Liddy blush. Before the 2010 ING NYC Marathon, Steph and I trained together, carbo-loaded together, and prayed together. She was the first person with whom I spoke upon staggering into the Team For Kids 2010 rendezvous point at Central Park's Cherry Hill. Perhaps more than anyone except my wife, Steph fully understood what the 2011 ING NYC Marathon meant to me.

Indiana Basketball Hall of Fame Board Member Graham Honaker, a solid distance runner, is among the most adept networkers I know. A professional who selflessly operates on the presumption of "yes," Graham provided continuous encouragement and material support throughout the writing and editing phases of this project.

Sid and Asteria Howard may be the only individuals more enthused about *Negative Splits* than me.

Brother Sid, a fellow Jersey Boy, and his bride are distance running's First Couple and the finest ambassadors of this sport. Period. With remarkable humility and unbounded enthusiasm, they inspire youth runners, train adult novice marathoners, and promote active living among seniors. Their unqualified support for this work convinced me of the merit of the undertaking.

I never knew either of my grandfathers. In the dark days before Major League Baseball® free agency and its life-changing wealth, Mom's father, Charles, declined the opportunity to become a Big League pitcher. While the Fort Lee (NJ) Department of Public Works was decidedly less glamorous than the National Pastime, it reliably put food on his growing family's table.

On the paternal side of my lineage, the original David White was a square-jawed New York City Police Officer who began our family's multi-generational commitment to serve and to protect. In 1930, Police Commissioner Grover Aloysius Whalen honored him as an elite member of the NYPD who modelled "courtesy, initiative, and good deportment." Mourners at his funeral filled the Church of St. Paul the Apostle on Manhattan's West Side. *Fidelis Ad Mortem.*

I would have been humbled to meet those great men.

My paternal grandmother, Frances, was a young widow who worked several jobs to care for her children. One of those engagements was housekeeper to His Eminence, Terrence Cardinal Cooke. On my best day, I have never exhibited an iota of her resolve.

My maternal grandmother, Margaret, served as Police Matron in Fort Lee and was responsible for processing female arrestees. Protective and kind, she possessed humor that would light up a room.

They remain with me in spirit. I am confident they take pride in their grandson's accomplishment.

Several friends have gone on to their heavenly reward much too soon. At day's end, we all cross life's Finish Line. Some simply start in an earlier wave.

My in-laws, Tom and Lynn, and their daughter, Julie, have long supported Jennifer and me in our Eastern Pennsylvania running exploits. Thanks to their hospitality, I know that "Keystone State" competitions will include a hot shower, a hearty post-race meal, and a bed in which to sneak 40 winks.

I offer the ultimate thanks to my Mom and Dad, Bernice P. and John F.X. White. From Little League® Baseball diamonds to township soccer pitches and unheated ice hockey rinks, they supported my various childhood athletic endeavors.

While all too often unspoken, my love for you is unwavering. I remain your grateful son.

ABOUT THE AUTHOR

David M. White is a law professor and licensed attorney. He earned a Bachelor of Arts Degree in Philosophy, a Masters in Liberal Studies, and a Juris Doctorate from Fordham University.

Professor White has innovated and instructed courses at the Georgetown University Law Center, the Fordham University School of Law, and the Yeshiva University Benjamin N. Cardozo School of Law. The Seton Hall University School of Law recognized him as its *Clinical Professor of the Year* (2014).

An avid endurance athlete, the author is a veteran of 3 marathons (New York City, Bermuda, and Harrisburg, PA) and 44 half marathons. He has won awards at various road and trail racing distances, and earned USA Track & Field recognition as a Masters All-American in the 5k, 5-Mile, 10k and Half Marathon events.

He resides in Manhattan with his wife, Jennifer, and their canine children, Katy and Hollister.